COUNTRY-SIDE MOOD

BLANDFORD PRESS
LTD.
16 WEST CENTRAL ST.
LONDON, W.C.1

Printed in Great Britain by Sydenham & Co. (Est. 1840) Ltd., Bournemouth

CONTENTS

COMPILED BY RICHARD HARMAN

Illustrations by Joan Rickarby

FOREWORD

IN an age of destruction there is a re-awakened interest in the things that endure. The hills, fields and rivers of England touch the hearts of all of us because they offer normal living and the natural joys of earth. Life is very much more real and full as we get close to the earth.

Our deepest attachment may be to one district ; it may happen that we feel we are part of the place we know best, or we may rejoice in the beauty everywhere.

The picture of England stored in most minds is the serene, satisfying countryside, and one of the most moving addresses broadcast in 1943 well illustrates how the thoughts of men in the Forces turn back to these things for strength and inspiration. It was given by Lieut.-Comdr. Peter Scott, who, in the course of the B.B.C. postscript on Easter Day, said :—

"Friday was St. George's Day. St. George for England. I suppose the 'England' means something slightly different to each of us. You may, for example, think of the white cliffs of Dover, or you may think of a game of bowls on Plymouth Hoe, or perhaps a game of cricket at Old Trafford or a game of rugger at Twickenham. But probably for most of us it brings a picture of a certain kind of countryside, the English countryside. If you spend much time at sea, that particular combination of fields and hedges and woods that is so essentially England seem to have a new meaning.

"I remember feeling most especially strongly about it in the late Summer of 1940 when I was serving in a destroyer doing anti-invasion patrol in the Channel. About that time I think everyone had a rather special feeling about the word 'England.' I remember as dawn broke looking at the black outlines of Star Point to the northward and thinking suddenly of England in quite a new way—a threatened England that was in some way more real and more friendly because she was in trouble. I thought of the Devon countryside lying beyond that black outline of the cliffs ; the wild moors and rugged tors inland and nearer the sea, the narrow winding valleys with their steep green sides ; and I thought of the mallards and teal which were rearing their ducklings in the reed beds of Slapton Leigh. That was the countryside we were so passionately determined to protect from the invader."

Who would not be England's champion? Who, having seen the changing beauties of the seasons, known something of her comeliness and grandeur or experienced the serenity and exhilaration which she can give, has not come to adore this fragment of God's creation?

But that is not all we associate with England in our deepest feelings. Set right across the scene there is the romantic legacy left to us by history and the time-honoured traditions found in rural life. These things, and the quality of the individual lives which have built up the national character, constitute the England we hold in our deepest thoughts and affections. Always, these are the simple things—the unspoiled scenes, the simple lives, the steadfast homes, and the unshakable faith.

All those who have England on their hearts can be grateful for the new return to the land. Fields that had fallen into disuse are again proudly displaying the even furrows of the plough. Farmsteads that were neglected are busy centres of man and beast. England has become a well-kept land again. Of the evidence that her soul is being reborn this is perhaps the strongest. Two contributors in the following pages tell something of their adventures in setting about the reclamation of the soil. A recent stay on one farm showed me a new motive for industry in this modern age. There was a spiritual impetus behind the farmer and the workers. They had welded themselves into a true community. Every one of them had a conviction that the tending of the earth is a sacred trust. They placed their labours on the highest plane, that of service to God for whom no standard of work is worthy but perfection. It may be that the land will lead the way in demonstrating to the industrial world how it may achieve a new spirit.

This book sets out a selection of works by authors who are intimate with the true England and who can pass on something of their experiences to the reader. The object has been to give a glimpse of the distinctive and satisfying riches which England offers to those who can absorb them with a searching and unhurried mind.

July, 1943. RICHARD HARMAN.

MEETING A MAN WITH
A HORSE-RAKE

By Adrian Bell

HAVING obtained a permit for timber for a shed (however many buildings one has, there is always one too few), for a sort of shanty, partly to house a few calves, partly for some corn, I catch Brisk and harness him to the spring cart one bright March morning, note thin front shoes—must take him to the blacksmith, too. Away we go. But no, wait—woa ! He takes a tightening of the rein to mean gee-up, as a spirited horse does. There is Nora at the door, waving something. What ? Woa, can't you ? Oh yes, I remember—the doll for Anthea's birthday. It is an old doll, really. It was a present for her second birthday. It was a rattling parcel ; it rattled as we turned it over to undo it. Then out came the doll, plump, waxen and flaxen; but, alas, she had no eyes; they were rattling about in her head, while she stared at us with vivid, fearful darkness. Anthea had many other presents, so we laid the doll aside, and wrote a polite letter of thanks. Now, in the fourth year of war, toyless, the peace-time doll will be a rare gift, if only the eyes can be fixed. So I am to take her into a shop where they have a reputation for mending dolls; a sort of dolls' hospital.

Now we are really off in the spring cart, with the doll and a rope and a horse collar to be repaired. I fancy she still rattles as we bounce over a dried clod left from the sugar-beet carting. As we round a bend, there approaches from the opposite direction a farmer with a horse-rake. I wonder what he has been doing with a horse-rake in March. We happen to meet at his farmyard gate. We stop, we pass the time of day. " Staunch pony you've got there. They say you never see a bad pony with a white nose."

There is a broken wall by a pond; it is a great gaping hole in a building, the bricks all lie in the water. A stack-cloth hoisted across to stop the gap has been blown out by the wind, torn to tatters. An old woman comes round a corner of the building, with a few withered-looking twigs in her hand. Her figure is white with the whiteness of bleached apron and snowy hair in the dry March sunlight. She is about to ask her son for something, but another thing gets the better of her. She turns to me, her mouth working. " Fifty years—we've been here fifty years." She stretches out her hands with the withered twigs. " Fifty years—and now we've got to have a sale. It's hard. All the stock we've bred ourselves. My dairy and butter-making . . . " Standing in the sunlight, larks singing, a little white old woman against the jagged broken wall.

" You make butter still? " Strange it is to find someone making butter these days. " Oh yes, I've forty registered customers. See my dairy."

Brisk, will you stand a minute? If you run off and

break that doll ——. It is all right, he has found a patch of forward grass. Here is her dairy, white as she, with a row of wide, shallow earthenware pans all round on a shelf. " It's skimmed, not separated—as good as some new. We sell it all." In a corner, with a clean cloth draped over it, is the churn, an old barrel churn, not even an end-over-end one. This dairy might be a hundred years ago. I have passed it almost daily without knowing.

But why this selling up after fifty years ? Outside now, the man takes up the tale. Hundreds of pounds-worth of ditching and draining must be done. He can't afford it all at once ; but in the interests of food production the Committee insist it must be undertaken. The Committee are not actually ousting him from his house or livelihood. He is to remain and work for them. He will be allowed to keep one cow for milk for his family. But the horses, the colts, the sheep, the cows, the heifers, the calves—all these that he bred himself are to be dispersed. Should he be able to get things together again to make a new start on his own one day, he asks ? His son, now, of twelve ; he wants him to be a farmer, and he is just getting interested in it.

The grandmother still stands motionless, halted in her quest of bill-hook by the broken wall.

But—and the sight of her standing there is like some dramatic moment, symbolic, against the broken wall—of what ?

" But," I exclaim, as something begins to glimmer in my mind, " say somebody bought this place from the landlord (it has been for sale, you say), and agreed to pay for all that ditching and draining, and farm it well ? Would they let him—let me—do it ? So that you needn't have a sale, and you could help me farm it . . . "

We all stare at one another. Nobody knows ; but it is a gleam. Now, what have I said ? " Well, you can have a look round and welcome," he says. Brisk is over the patch of grass, and soon one wheel will be in the ditch. We unhitch him in a moment. Mr. Groves bustles two big colts (or three, it is dark and they are dark) out of a shed by a further door, and leads Brisk in. Takes

and lays at his feet an armful of crisp brown clover hay.
Brisk is nervous of him and of the shed—but, ah, this is
good, he says in a sniff. We leave him, with a gleam
in his eye, champing a moustache-shaped bunch of it.

Sad, dour, heavy land, bricky-hard on top and dank
below. Oh, how much needs to be done here ; the power
even beyond horses' strength it is crying out for, to rip
up the bushes and thorns, and regenerate fields from
thickets. Yet the man loves his land ; it is just that,
without help, it has got beyond him. The stock alone
is one person's job. Every shed is full of cattle ; sheep
run to his wife bringing them kale in the meadow. Four
plough horses stand in the stable. A pony puts its nose
through a gap in weatherboarding. Geese honk, calves
bleat, dogs bark, and a crowd of children are playing
round the door. The yards are hollow. (" Like saucers,"
I tell Nora later. " Like basins," she says when she sees
them, " —of soup.")

So we put Brisk in the cart again, and I go on my way.
Such are the unforeseen interruptions to a journey to
town.

The timber merchant's yard is by the river. He and
I discuss matters unconnected with timber—Tolstoy's
" War and Peace," and what it is that makes a misty day
in November among flat fields, when he sits down to
sketch it, something more than mist and fields and hedges.
The way you see it—the way God sees it ; the way I watch
my little Sylvia shelling beans, utterly preoccupied as
white wonder of bean after bean tinkles out of the golden
pods ; going on and on, wordless, while I stare, tired,
in the act of taking off my boots. The way I love, yes
already, that dour, sour land for the good thing it might be.

I return up the street from the river with the white
new timber, such as it is. William, who knows all about
timber, being a carpenter, will not think much of it. But
" you were lucky to get it " is the opinion of friends
I meet, and I think so too. Will Brisk stand a minute
outside the doll shop, while I call for—but she hasn't
yet a name—with her eyes in ? A friend happens to meet
me just there, who has a barn which he does not want,

not being a farmer, which threatens to blow down piece-meal, pantiles and old timbers with the ivy curling in between. An old tithe barn; he would sell it to me almost for a fiver. But how to move it? No, I must build with crude new fir. "Be a good fellow and stand by Brisk a minute." There is the doll; they have put her eyes in all right, though there is a slight cast in the left one. But something now has happened to her body. It has shrunk. No, they have had to detach head from body to get at the eyes, and have stuck the head on the wrong body, which is much too small. I cannot take home that pigmy grotesque. "Oh, how silly of me," cries the harassed doll-mender, and there is a hasty reassembly.

Two telephone calls. Any chance of being allowed to farm that farm if I bought it? The possibility is distant, faint and feminine, from a Committee secretary. There is just a thread of possibility. Again my money goes tinkling into the box (I have chosen the kiosk beside the road half-way home, where Brisk is within reach of my hand, I half in, half out of it—there is a good length of flex, luckily). "Hullo. Yes, it is for sale. It's cheap, though I have never been able to persuade anybody else so. You can have a week to think it over."

Jogging home on the timber, I reach the downward slope to the brook. I have never concerned myself much with the view beyond before, but now—there lies the land of Groves Farm spread out. We turn past the buildings. Harry Groves is coming out of his barn; he stops me. He has found the particulars, with map, in an old sale catalogue, when they tried to sell the farm along with the rest of the estate years back. Would I come in a minute? The children are all home from school and hungry for tea, crowded round the square kitchen table. The youngest, Alice, not yet two, toddles to the door and puts up a hand to try to stroke Brisk's nose, who is looking in also. A lamp already casts a glow in the shadowy room. Mother is cutting bread and butter, grandmother pouring out milk. I see out of the corner of my eye the knife moving again and again across the loaf; it never seems to stop, and grandmother is pouring out always. "This is Billy—he's going to be a farmer; he'll help in his holidays. This is Dorry." A large-scale map eclipses both their teas. Father's finger moves about it, dark like a little plough; mother's knife glints, crossing the loaf yet again; grandma's jug is refilled. I am trying to take in what father is saying, eyes following the finger till they slip off it to find where a field should be, the flaxen blue-eyed face of little Alice craning up at me in seraphic curiosity. "That's grown up with bushes now," father is saying. What? Where? I have lost the finger; it is at the other end of the farm. Billy and Dorry are groping for and going on with their tea under the map, which keeps moving draughtily. "There—you take it." I put it under my arm. All the dogs bark again as I start off through the yard, and that makes the sheep bleat, and the cows moo. The whole farmyard is mooing, barking, bleating, under the evening star. Another star flickers out as with infectious agitation.

At home, all unloaded, animals fed and our tea over, I go into my room with an armful of brushwood and the map. The twins run in crying, "We want to make some firelight."

"Let me bellow it." "No, it's my turn." Ash flies; firelight leaps up. They stand and admire it, watching it dance on walls and ceiling. Then Sylvia looks at the floor. "Father, why do you keep your room so dusty and dirty?" "Do you mean the hearth?" I ask. (They have scattered ash and embers.) "No, the splintery part of the floor, too."

"What a lot of books you've got. Oh, here's a cutting-out book." (It is an old Army and Navy Stores catalogue.) "Did you use to cut out in this book when you were a little boy?" The book is extracted and carried off between them. But they do not get far with it. I hear them on the stairs. "It's got some lovely things in it."

I spread the map and the sale particulars out on my table under the lamp. The folio is dated 1925, and the title of the estate, on the cover, is in Gothic lettering. I turn to Groves Farm. "A very Desirable Holding.

Stabling for four horses—open-bay shed." (" That'll be the one that has fallen into the pond " Nora says, who has come in and is reading over my shoulder.)

Next day come more up-to-date particulars from the agent. This folio is dated 1940, when they last tried to sell the farms. This time the lettering is plain ; Groves Farm has become " A Handy-sized Holding."

William is outside looking at the timber I brought home. He smiles wryly to think what things are coming to. " Why," he says, " the scantling you used to get when your house was built, you could make a ladder of. Father made several of it ; this is one." He jumps on it as it leans against the house, to show the strength. " Good as oak. Look at the sills of your house ; as sound as when they were put in. As long as you keep it painted, it will last for ever."

" But we are lucky to get anything, these days."

With spade, foot rule, hammer and nails, we propose to erect our shanty. We are not relying on the " home-grown " fir, as invoiced, for strength. We have oak posts cut from these hedgerows, that have been leaning up into the big oak tree for the past year, awaiting an occasion for their use. So we measure by paces, and put in little sticks, and alter them, and pace about, till we think we have got it right. Then we dig, and ram in the posts ; nail a cross-piece. Is it horizontal ? In turn we look at it from a distance, and tell the other to raise it a bit that end, or the further end. Neither of us can really quite agree about it. We measure ; but that makes it look unbelievably slanting. In the end we compromise between his idea of dead-level and mine. That oak bough that cuts across our view of it, and waves in the wind, puts us off, we agree. Thenceforth the building becomes frankly approximate, conditioned by the natural deviations of the oak posts. William shows much native ingenuity in making the various inward and outward curves come within our rectangle. In some cases nothing can be done but make a false frame of scantling to square the timbers, just as a surface for nailing. William enjoys this kind of building, working the growing shapes into a plan. And every time he has settled the problem of a corner, and chiselled a way to mortise square deal into rough oak, he hammers in five inch nails with ringing blows that allow of no doubting or undoing.

For a roof nothing is procurable but tin. No hope of tiles, unless I unroofed my friend's barn. We have not enough timber to make a basis for roofing felt. And even tin is not galvanized any longer, and goes rusty in a night. I had overlooked this, and am without anything to paint it with for a day or two. In that time the whole roof goes brick-red with rust. The yet unpainted fir looks white and raw. Altogether, it is a horror, and Nora tells me so. Only the shape is not bad ; she concedes that. But I stand in the building at dusk, listening to rain tinkling down on the roof, sharing shelter with the ladder, a saw and a few other tools, and think that a roof, just any roof, is good, especially to farmers who endure so much spoilation by the weather. The tinkling of those drops that cannot now reach these square yards of ground is music to me.

Nora, this evening, is busy stitching tiny garments for the doll with the restored eyes, though real garments are also urgently needed, as always. She has to stop every now and then to exclaim, " Lovely stuff this is, just feel it." Scraps of the past, of peace-time garments. Dolls are better clad than humans now.

We are looking again at the map of Groves Farm. It is shaped rather like an X, the fields fanning out on either side of the house and buildings. But the electric light keeps flickering. Martin blinks his eyes and says, " Did you see that one ? " Anthea has an idea about it. " My believance is —— " she begins, but then the light goes right out. We grope for candles.

One candle and firelight in my room. A glowing excuse not to write the letters I owe, but sit and read for a quarter of an hour, oaken candlestick balanced on the arm of my chair, Massingham on the implicit compact between man and nature. And here am I building with tin and unseasoned fir. But one must be thankful even for tin. Then a gloaming supper, and we sit and talk.

But suddenly the technicians switch life on again. Candles and conversation—electric light and account books and newspapers.

The shanty is finished; creosote has turned the crude wood silky brown; the big oak tree hides most of the roof. We go to cart a little stack of hay home to it, out of Mr. Sonning's orchard. Brisk dislikes the rustle of hay behind him even more than he dislikes the roadman in the hedge, or the flash of his shovel, or his tricycle draped with a sack. Even his appetite for early grass at his feet will not make him forget it. He stands uneasily, while I climb on the cart to load the hay. We have nearly a load, and I am just saying to William, "He is getting used to it," when he catches sight of me above him, over the top of his blinkers. Away we go at a canter. I just miss being beheaded by Mrs. Sonning's linen line. The trees fly past, yet we hit none, and while I am thinking what to do (it does not take long in that position), we miraculously clear the gateway into the next meadow. Often I have thought, passing through that meadow, how badly it needs draining. Now I am thankful that the winter's rains still stand there; a wet Suffolk meadow is the best place in which to be run away with. Not even Brisk can gallop along with a load of hay in it. I slide off the load, fall softly, and running, overtake him.

It is a Saturday; the news of the runaway quickly gets to the children of the village, and they come running, to see if it will happen again. By the afternoon a crowd of them are playing round our diminishing stack. The eldest tires of this, and takes a fork and seeks to help. We take him back with us to the shed, and push him in between the hay and the roof, and there he scrambles about, packing it in tight. Nora brings us tea whose steam is blown horizontal in the nipping east wind, and an apple and piece of cake for the boy. He says, as we take Brisk out of the shafts, "When I leave school I'll come and work for you."

We have a considerable heap of hay left over, despite his efforts. This we stack against the end of the building. Around and over this is erected a piece of real rickety

Suffolk improvization. I know I shall be ashamed of it to-morrow, but now it is starting to sleet; anything to keep out the weather. William aids. We arrange three unused (alas, also unpainted) sheets of tin over it, supported by the big nut-bush at one end. A length of deal nailed with one nail to an elm pole leaning against it, supports the roof. One piece of tin we bend over to shield the end. "We want a crotched piece to put under it." I find a crotched piece ("leave one crotch long"), and we jam it underneath. "We can tie that corner with a bit of string." The stack-cloth is hung over the front, and a sack weighted by a stone curtains a gap across which the cloth would not quite reach.

"We shall need another pole jammed in here to tie the stack-cloth back to." More jamming, thrusting and scraping of wood on tin. It is trying to snow now. Only one corner is left exposed. "We can put some bushes to fill that." William grasps thorn bushes cut from the hedge, and crushes them into the corner with the weight of his body, shouldering them, sitting on them. "Thorns'll catch a lot of driving snow. Wonderful what a lot of snow a few thorn bushes'll catch." So there it is—a sort of rustic tabernacle built round the hay, a rough sketch of a building done with a nail and a bit of string.

"You can hang an old bag across the doorway if the weather drives in," William says, in parting for the day. I vow I won't, to myself. Yet to-morrow, Sunday, comes, and the sleet is driving from the south-east, and I do go and hang that old bag. "It looks as though we've turned gipsy," Nora says, coming back from church. Yet the hay, the precious hay, is safe.

We endure this flapping, tattered, tent-like structure for a week; then on Sunday a hurricane blows up, and blows it all away. Anthea has discovered a new book, *Poems of To-day*, and is oblivious of the gale. Away go the sheets of tin like sheets of paper, into the middle of the wheat field. Slates are lifting off the goat's stall. I drag bricks, logs, anything heavy, up on the roof to weight them down, even an old wireless battery. Then

resting by the fire, while Anthea reads to me, " I will
make you brooches, and toys for your delight." Another
crash, and away goes the tin again, scattering the young
tree trunks I had laid on them. Brisk stares anxiously
from his stable ; a slate hurtles down, nearly cutting off
his nose. Bang goes the top door in his face. The goat is
terrified by the wind flapping in the sacks hung over her
slatted window. I fasten a board outside. More poetry
by the fire with Anthea. So the day roars away.

It has wrecked the makeshift shelter over the hay,
abolished it. That is a good thing. I gather up the
poles, string, sacks ; collect what of the hay did not
follow the tin into the wheat, and leave the " hovel," as
William calls it, tidy and decent. " Not a bad hovel,"
he says, not in any sense of detraction. " We didn't get
that roof-tree quite level after all ; I could see as soon
as I came into the gateway this morning. We didn't go
back far enough from it, to look."

Never mind, it withstood the gale. I am chopping
sticks and logs inside ; the wind has sunk, there is a
young moon. I always forget the chores until dusk ; but
there would not be time for them before. Where is the
former Suffolk back-door boy (back-'us boy) ? On
the aerodrome, or learning to drive the tractor plough.
(Only this morning I was told of a young naval candidate
who went very nervously for an interview with a
great man. He found him on hands and knees, lighting
his own fire.) The sticks go bounding about as I chop,
some even to the roof—ting ! One to my eye. I see
in my mind's eye, the other one, the old white woman
against the sunny broken wall murmuring, " Fifty years,
fifty years." I see again another old lady in the village
shop, saying, " My mother nursed his mother when she
was having him. It's hard." This village solidarity
cemented by time, though often all that is apparent is a
number of little tiffs. " IT " is to blame. Not even
" They." Lack of labour, lack of capital, lack of prospect.
Shall I succeed where he has failed ? Or will Nora one
day be coming round the corner by the wall in the March
sunlight sighing, " Fifty years—it is hard " ?

What am I letting myself in for? A farm? A farm is one thing, but what is this? I go over it of evenings, giving the ground a kick which jams my toe hard against my boot, but does not budge or break the furrow. Fifteen acres of it are wilderness. "That's all grown up with bushes," Harry Groves was saying of it, as his work-dark finger moved on to certain green spaces of the map, the 1925 map. The 1940 map has little dots sprinkled about that portion. Those are the bushes. It is the first time I have seen land deterioration shown on a map. It was almost frightening up there, primeval, tumbledown thicket not woodland. But then, coming down to the farmyard, I found myself face to face with Harry beside his last stack who was saying, "If you farm it, and set me to plough, and bring me out the second pair of horses at midday, I'd not stop for dinner. Just a bite of bread and cheese as I stand . . ."

And suddenly there is heart to put heart into that land.

The low, square dunghills grow in size on Groves Farm; every day Harry Groves is at work with horse and tumbril getting out the manure for valuation. This is the last act of his tenancy. One evening I come to him after yet another walk round, with the cart tipped up against the dunghill by the stackyard, forking out the last load. "We might," I suggest, "if they let me know in time, get a start here together next week." He agrees. Everything is settled except wages; we must get them fixed. He is telling me the story of the odd duck among his dozen, a wild one really, that came one morning and settled on the pond among them. Then it flew off to a thicket where there was another pond. A man who hired the shooting of the farm appeared just then, and Harry told him, "There's a wild duck just flown over the thicket." The man went off, and returned shortly, saying, "I shot that duck, but then I remembered that that pond and thicket don't belong to this farm. It fell into the pond; I couldn't get it." Harry went later, and found the duck on the edge of the pond with its head down as though dead. He picked it up, and found that it was not dead. In fact, it only seemed to have one shot in it, through the neck. He took it home, put it in a coop and fed it on slops, and it recovered. When the sportsman came again, Harry said, " There's your duck, but don't go and shoot it again."

But I am thinking of wages ; what to offer. Enough to avoid the vexing business of keeping count of hours of overtime. " I'll work for you as I'd work for myself," he has said. That's it, a sum to cover Sunday work with cows and feeding horses, and evening hours in the field. We are in the dark stable now, the chestnut mare trying to turn about to see where the food is coming from. Standing beside the great bodies of the horses, I make my offer—actually to the seat of Harry Groves' trousers, as he dives deep into the chaff bin, which is nearly empty. A bit more than the farm can stand in its present state, I know ; and yet he is going to work all hours . . .

He recovers from the chaff bin, and stands quiet in the darkness. A daughter calls, " I can't undo the halter of the blue cow." " All right—I'll come." And then, slowly, " You don't want to pay me as much as that. As long as we can keep our few fowls, and have some milk, and live in the house—that's worth something."

Indoors, having his tea, with the oil lamp just alight, the lean face in profile becomes somehow timeless. His wife standing over him pouring out his tea, grannie nursing little Alice who is finishing her milk, eldest boy coming in with a box of kindling wood. " We only want to live," she says, endorsing her husband's words. " We've had to do on a good deal less than that in our time." " We only want to live," grannie echoes.

The following morning I am in telephone conversation with Harry Groves' valuer. " Without prejudice to my client's interests," he is saying. I reply (I am learning the right phrases), " It is understood from the executive officer that the Committee would have no objection to the course I propose."

What a number of wheels two pennies tinkling into a telephone box can start turning. Many are the plans

I have made in the past that have come to nothing ; and then, meeting a man coming round a corner with a horse dragging a rake, and wondering idly what he had been doing with a horse-rake in March . . .

That was three weeks ago. Since then I have learned much of how England is run, of how suddenly, after twenty years of neglect and ruination, a government of good husbandry is set up and functions, ostensibly in committee rooms, actually in fields and farmhouse parlours, in homely, practicable advice from one farmer to another. Till Suffolk begins to look again as I first remember it, when I came to " the best farm in Benfield " nearly twenty-five years ago, to me then just a level expanse of bare earth. What gives me good hope of rural England is that when Farmer Brown becomes a committee-man, he remains Farmer Brown.

In the old days it was simply a matter of having the capital that allowed one to handle this earth. It is by no means so to-day. Which gives one a proper sense of responsibility. If any such reminder were necessary, it was before my eyes as I journeyed yesterday through the lands of a large estate. Not only the fields, but the woods, the hedgerow timber, every tree, had a look of being tended. All had a sober yet singing order that was like art ; it *was* art, the greatest. And the horses, harrows, drills, tractors, moving about the landscape were its breathing and its life. It was a picture that drew the past to the present, both were knit in it. The great estate, its every house a home, integral to it, seemed to me then England's very nature.

After these comings and goings, I am sitting again on the chopping-block in my hovel, calves penned on my left, hay piled on my right, waiting for the last hen to go to roost. I am moving towards something new, yet I feel very still, solidly set on this chopping-block in my home acres. This hovel has become something too, in this little while ; a place of rumination into which the sun and moonlight come. The oaken posts give it power ; a man might quite simply pray here, at this chopping-block. Or think, staring at the wide eye of a laying hen which stares as fixedly back. The hens have taken to it; they have two nests, under the hay and upon it; some lay upstairs, some down. Hay-bowls of eggs which I empty daily. It is a place in which to wait, in which to think; while the post-girl comes each morning, and the postman takes the letters each night, and pieces of paper come to me with figures upon them, and pieces of paper go from me with figures upon them, moving me all the time, unobtrusively as an hour hand, from the placing of those actual coins in the box, towards farming that dour, sour land. To the four horses in the stable (one a Suffolk colt, coming five, not yet been to plough), the two yearlings in the yard, seven cows in the neat-house, five heifers in the field, calves in all the pens, twenty sheep (and a marsh for summer grazing on the Waveney). The days are fine and dry now, my neighbours have nearly all finished drilling, though March is only half-way through. But Groves Farm waits half-ploughed, unsown, undrained, till the legal word is given.

Suddenly, then, any day now, it will be ploughing, harrowing, drilling, tractor-cultivating, from light till dark. By any and every means that land must be restored. Still there will be Sundays, or portions of Sundays, and corners of quiet, in which I can return to my hovel, even as my old farmer friend, Mr. Colville, used to go to his seat in the wood when he wanted to think and plan, sitting so still that the wild birds and the foxes came near.

A DEVON STREAM

By HENRY WILLIAMSON

I

ONE Summer day, motoring from London to Devon in my old Silver Eagle sports car, I stopped beside a chalk stream in Wiltshire, and knelt down on the bank. An idea to alter the character of a Devon stream, wherein I fished at home, had come into my head.

Pulling a string of water-crowfoot, or river buttercup, from its root, I saw how numerous were the nymphs and larvae of ephemeral flies crawling on the green leaves, and fresh-water shrimps flipping along the stems. If only I could make my own little river so full of trout-food, what fish would I see there in the years to come ! Instead of trout of a quarter of a pound, which was the average weight, I might be catching pounders and even two-pounders on my red-hackle flies. Keen with this idea, I bought a pail from the village shop and, pulling more weed from the stream, put it in the pail with water, and headed for the remote West Country.

When I got home, I waded in the river and planted lengths of the crowfoot under stones, spaced in different runs and eddies. I had little hope that the weed would grow, for I had been told that the spates of the rough moorland stream would tear them away as fast as they grew—if indeed they did grow. Yet I hoped they would grow, to provide shelter for trout-food, and also for the trout. If any eggs of flies were on the leaves, I doubted if *they* would thrive ; for water from the peat-beds of the moor was, I knew, acid, while a chalk stream is alkaline.

During the first Winter, after the succession of spates had run down the wooded valley to the sea, and when the water was clear again, so that it was a pure delight to stare at the stones and shillets of the river bed, coloured grey and brown and blue in the sunshine, I saw with anxiety that every green bine or string, each laid so carefully under a flat stone the Summer before, was buried. Yet, as the Spring days increased and the water ran clearer and lower, I saw with delight that tresses of bright green were waving in the planted places. They grew longer, until in Summer white flowers of crowfoot were lying on the water.

When the rains came and the stream rushed turbid and grey, the silt and sand buried them, for the tresses made stopping places in the bed of the river. They were smothered, I thought, as spate after spate thundered over the waterfalls where salmon and sea-trout, eager for the spawning beds of gravel on the moor, were leaping and trying to swim up in the white surge of the waters.

Yet once again in Spring the plants grew bright and green with an amazing luxuriance. The silt had buried them in the Autumn ; and in the Spring the buried strings had put forth white rootlets, which had pushed into the silt, binding it, and causing more silt and gravel to lodge there. And during the third season, when the lusty sunshine of another West Country Spring broke through Atlantic clouds, the solid-spread plants put forth white feelers, or roots, a hundredfold, each seeking the sunshine through the cold clear water. The sun gave each discoverer a green fringe ; and soon the long tendrils were waving and swaying in the rippled water-flow. They gave cover for trout, and was it only my imagination that there now seemed to be double the rises during the evening ?

During the fourth Spring the sight of so many weeds began to give me uneasy thoughts. The river was indeed changing. Then someone told me of the Welsh river Clwyd, which had been ruined by a few bits of Canadian pondweed being planted in its upper waters. In imagination I saw " my " river (I was only the tenant of a beat of about two miles) ruined by a clotted mass of weed, spreading in geometric progression all the way down to the tide-head. I saw a score of fishermen, with sixteen-foot double-handed rods, gazing with chagrin at their favourite runs and salmon pools, all choked by hundreds of tons, thousands of tons, of matted water-crowfoot weeds. The vision persisted ; until early one morning, unable to bear the burden of my guilt any longer, I got out of bed, put on my clothes, fishing stockings, waders, and brogues ; and with rake, mattock and scythe, went forth into the water-dim dawn to begin my work of removing every bit of weed from the river.

By noon I had realized why the claws of a Devon otter's front paws are usually worn down. The gravel had worn my finger-nails to the quick. Abandoning scythe, mattock and rake after the first five minutes, I had worked to pull the weed from the river bed with my hands. At once the sleeves of my coat and shirt were wet ; and pausing to straighten my aching back, time after time, resting with hands on lower ribs, my shirt and trousers were soon dripping.

Hour after hour I hauled armfuls of dripping weed to float away in the current. The water had long ago filled my waders. At last, as the sun was setting among the trees, I went home to eat; but not to rest and feel that good work had been done, for I had cleared only a small part of the weed-beds, and even so, the roots were still embedded in their shoals of silt.

Every bit must be uprooted, not merely the outer and visible strings removed. I started again the next morning, at dawn. Day after day I toiled in the river. At last it was all gone—at least visibly. The forester of the saw mills below my beat complained that his waterwheel was choked with the stuff.

That was a year or two ago. Meanwhile I had left Devon, and gone to farm in Norfolk.

I returned there in the Summer before the war. I walked on the banks and saw my beds of water buttercup in flower. It was a beautiful sight. Islets of gravel stood out of the low Summer level of the river. Fast runs of crystal water hurried between the islets, rippling water bright with oxygen. Nymphs of the olive dun were hatching, and small trout were taking them. I saw many lipping rises. The water was alive with them. Wading in, I lifted the weed, to find the long green strings crawling with caddis and shrimp. A trout well over a foot long zigzagged away from my white feet. How vain and precipitant had been my panic, my premonition of a ruined river!

I saw how the islets had formed in what before was a slow, level, somewhat dull stretch of water. The weed had grown fastest in this stretch, and had collected the most silt. As the silt increased, so the weeds increased, until they formed shoals in the Winter stream. As the water fell, so the shoals became islets. The exposed weed on the islets died away, and between the islets the currents ran faster. And running fast, the currents or streams began to undercut the islets, making hiding places for fish; and, slowly, reducing the islets.

Fish lurked there in the keener water made brighter by its swiftness. Also mayflies, which before had been scarce in the river (as there had been few silt beds in which the larvae could burrow), had increased and the trout were growing fat on them.

I learned that the new tenant of the fishing had had, during one evening, over sixty rises in that part of the river where before my little gamecock-hackle fly, with its three whisks of pheasant-tail tied with gilt wire, had seldom brought more than three fish to the creel.

II

For seven years, while I was living at the fishing cottage of Shallowford, it was my habit to walk along the river bank about noon, and return after about an hour's peering at trout, otter spraints (always on the same ant-hill, rock-ledge, and gravelly scour under the railway viaduct where apparently one old dog-otter used to enjoy himself by kicking out his hind legs), foot-marks of herons, pheasants, dabchicks, dippers, and other birds. The river was the Bray, a fast rock-and-gravel stream rising on Exmoor and joining the Mole, famous for its salmon, down the valley before coming to the big Taw and so to the Atlantic beyond Barnstaple and the estuary.

During the past five years I have been a farmer in East Anglia, and life has been concerned entirely with engines and ploughs, horses, cows and sheep, grass-cutters and files, bolts, nuts, grease, paraffin, ladders, sacks, the quality of barley, the tonnage of sugar beet, with hoeing, row-crop cultivation, windows, doors, paint, fencing, barb-wire, ring-worm, white scour in calves, wages' book and rates of overtime, and all the incessant materialistic details which make up the farming life. Somewhere under the silt of incessant detail the artistic consciousness lies buried—my other self, my former self. If my outward self is here in the east, my heart or spirit is away in the west, somewhere on the hills where once was freedom, and in the bright pure waters of the Bray.

Not that I found life always easy there, for I had grown up on the battlefields, and the years between the two wars were never truly peaceful. There was always some thing ghostly about life as I felt and sensed it ; something frustrated, something shut away, not perceived by others with whom I had my being—or part of my being. But when I turned to the water and the wild places of the moor, there I seemed to find truth, and that was why, I think, I was generally alone ; only part of myself was lived in the vicinity of other people.

The little green valley spanned by the Great Western Railway viaduct, with the oaks and spruce plantations on its steep sides, and the Bray running noisily over the stony shallows and pouring whitely down the falls, seems now to be myself as I was in the West Country. Those familiar stones and ledges and alder roots which my eyes saw day after day, year after year, were my life. They were me. Watching the same trout in the pools and runs, as I walked daily along the banks—some of the fish, indeed, remained there Summer after Summer— intensified the illusion that one day, when I was gone, the river would cease to be. It would be different. A common human illusion, I know ; an illusion that lies in every grave on earth. Yet when I, too, am gone from the face of the earth, perhaps part of this illusion of self will remain as a visible and actual thing for others ; for the feeling that I had is, I tell myself, secured in words, in the book called *Salar the Salmon*, into which I put all I knew of the river and its myriad and varying life. Even so, that book holds within its covers only a very small part of the river's life ; for one man's sight, and that inner sight called imagination, is puny in the comprehensive light-beams of the sun, the servant of the Creator.

* * * * *

I remember how, in my ignorance, I tried to alter the course and nature of the river. It was my ambition to make the pools deeper, to hold bigger trout than the river could feed. Some of the dams I made in the river will last a few years ; but only a few years.

I began this series of engineering works, in my ambitious ignorance, by getting about a hundred old potato sacks, a couple of tons of cement, a heavy pointed shovel called locally a " Welsh backbreaker," and an ordinary gardening barrow. I had an enthusiastic helper in a young woman who recently had come from London to help my literary career, accompanied by typewriter, shorthand books, filing cabinets, and a great bulk of pencils and paper. I was an author, and an author must have a secretary. Before very long, however, the pencil and notebook gave way to the " Welsh backbreaker " and the cement sack, and together we were intent on digging a dozen tons or so of gravel from the gravel ridges left by Winter floods. Valiantly this young lady, but lately a typist of the B.B.C., prodded hard gravel banks with the heavy shovel, shook stiff brown paper bags of cement into the barrow, or scooped pails of water from the river. The idea was to mix the " batch " in the barrow, shovel it into the potato sack held open at the stream's edge, until about a quarter of a ton of concrete bulged therein. When filled, the solid sack was heaved over, and trodden flat. When this was done, the centre of the sack was ripped open and flat stones were set upright into the wet concrete. A week or so later, when all had become solid, we heaved and pushed and levered, with crowbar and pick, the hard slabs into position, until a dam of stepping stones was made across the stream.

I learned a lot about water in those days—how usually it does the opposite of what the amateur engineer hopes it will do. To make more pools for trout to rest in, I thought, would be to have, eventually, more trout. But the river wanted its pools to be of its own fashioning, and immediately began to undo our work.

For a week or two, the dam certainly raised the level of the pool above it ; but every minute, every instant, the water was working to undo it. The flow was slower than before, and therefore more silt and sand and gravel was left behind the dam. After every spate, the pool bed was raised by the unmoving accumulation on its bed ; while the water pouring over the concrete slabs cut pits immediately below them. These pits deepened until the slabs had gradually slidden into them, filling them up ; and the quickening current began to disturb and to pass on the accumulation of silt, sand and gravel above the slabs. Where was my dam after the Winter's floods had gone down to the sea ? Buried under gravel—and the river flowing on serenely shallow as before !

We made six dams in all. One was at the tail of a pool, to deepen it, and to make under a great and ancient oak tree—four hundred years of growing there—a resting place for salmon. The dam altered the involved flowings of many currents which had caused the original cutting of the pool above—a circular pool which revolved—called the Wheel Pool. So the current ceased to revolve round the banks, and it looked somewhat dull and sullen, inactive. The river had begun to cut through the lower dam, and the middle parts were sunken ; even so, it made a nice fast run. Gradually the accumulation of sand and gravel was washed down to the next pool, making it shallower. Most of our work wasted ; hundreds of hours of back-ache, of heaving, pushing, levering, of icy-aching hands and arms and feet, of hands roughened and cracked with the lime in the cement—all wasted.

One of our six dams was successful. As I observed on my return just before the recrudescence of the World War, the river had accepted it. Trout rested above and below the slabs, which still bore the marks of the jute sacking. A heron was using one of the stones as a spearing stance for fish. That dam was put across a narrow, fast part of the river, under the old oak which must have stood there before Cromwell's men hacked off the apostolic pew-heads carved from its oaken ancestors which had been dragged into nearby churches. Once, when the water was crystal-clear after a spate, I saw a salmon lying there ; and crawling along a branch of the oak, I managed to photograph it. The photograph is lost, mildewed somewhere in the unpacked boxes in a barn of the Norfolk farm ; but I can still see myself staring with sudden joy into the waters below.

Under the old oak tree, in whose hollow travelling otters sleep, my dam remains to-day, the stream bubbling and swirling by it. Caddis larvae, which build for them-selves little houses of stick and gravel-speck, held together with their own cement, hide under the slabs. Trout dart under their shadow'd sanctuary when alarmed by beating grey heron wings, or fisherman's heavy-nailed boots moving upstream. I daresay it will last for a year or two before the slabs crumble. They were not really well made; too much silt in the gravel to bind stone and sand together, in order to withstand the everlasting abrasion of a gravel stream. For a river bed itself is alive, in constant motion, always in movement, cutting, dislodging, grinding, abrading, polishing—always shifting part of the earth's crust down to the sea. Nothing remains, except the spirit of the water. Trout and caddis, heron and eel, waving crowfoot flower of Summer, blue flash and lancing cry of kingfisher, stone-song of dipper, and man who regards them—these things pass, and are renewed, all animated awhile by the spirit which breathes on the face of the waters.

Knowing this, I cannot but be tranquil when, under the silting details of a business man's life—undertaken for the sake of four growing sons, who will help to make a Greater Britain wherein all men shall work for the fellowship of the community—I see in sudden poignancy of memory the little Bray river and the ghost of myself and the small children peering over the bridge; or recall the mystery of solitude by the riverside with rod and red-hackle fly at sunset when the red spinners were rising and falling over the pools and glides, while the evening star—which is also the morning star leading up another day—shines over the western hills.

A COUNTRY LANE

SOME MARSHLAND MEMORIES

By S. L. Bensusan

I

At first sight there was nothing really remarkable about
the road. It was merely beautiful, winding in restful
and inviting fashion between a double row of elm trees,
broken now and again by the brief hedge of a cottage
garden, the cottage Elizabethan or Jacobean at least,
with thatch or deep red tiles for roof, and a very big

cellar to which access was given by a trap door, so that a piece of carpet or a table with reasonably wide cloth might hide it from prying eyes. When I visited one of the cottages for the first time, in the brave days when I was twenty-one, there was no need to hide the cellar; smuggling had ceased to be a business, it had become a fragrant memory of joys in which parson, squire and peasant had a share.

As Father William, the oldest inhabitant, remarked to me once, after showing me a small and beggarly array of squat black bottles, all empty: "Git over me what th' lads are about nowadays. I count they got furrin parts over there still," and he pointed to the east across the estuary, "th' tides are still runnin' an' men still got mouths. But they'd liefer goo clammin' an' winklin' an' fishin' for dabs than run a few bottles across. I don't think nawthen' to sech an' that's th' truth. A man don't want a cellar nowadays. Telly f'r why; there ain't nawthen' to put in it excep' it's a cast o' beer, an' on'y Gran'feyther got th' money f'r that, darn him. I do hope th' dear Lord'll let me stay hereabouts long enough to see he quackle."

Gran'feyther had the first of the period cottages on the right as you walked up the road after leaving the Wheatsheaf. He was two or three years younger than Father William, five feet and one or two inches high; he wore a short grey beard, a blue jersey and gold wires in his ears. Everybody agreed that he had enjoyed more than a fair share of luck.

I remember the afternoon when Father William told me the story, sitting in his ingle nook, with the red and brown woollen capes over his coat and the so-called "shovel" hat that a parson now dead had given him. He kept it on his head indoors and out. "He ain't got a wife now, no more ain't Gran'feyther," he began, "no more than me. The dear Lord took mine an' He wore kindly welcome. There's some say a wife don't cost nawthen' but that's a lie. Vittles for one comes cheaper than vittles for two, an' a woman wants a bit o' dressin' whiles, an' time you've took your harvest money she 'members it.

If you're a widder man, you gotter clean an' cook f'r yersel, that's all. Mos' wimmen are too fond o' cleanin' things to my thinkin'. There's some'll wash plates an' cups every time they use 'em. But there; I wore tellin' ye about Gran'feyther.

"Three boys he had to be sure, mischieful young mucks, I ouldn't ha' give thrippence apiece f'r 'em. But one on 'em went on the rileway an' a traine run over him, an' th' rileway had to pay Gran'feyther f'rever o' money. An' that wornt two year arter that a brewer's horse run away and knocked another on 'em down an' killed him, an' them brewers pide Gran'feyther a lot o' money not to git 'em locked up. He bought that cottage he lives in, an' got a gre't cast o' beer in his cellar. An' the son what he got left is same as a seaman, an' comes here now an' agen with a pocketful o' money.

"He bin an' bought Gran'feyther a wondrous knit wool jarsey f'r th' cowd weather an' forever o' baccy. An' him rollin' in money an' drinkin' his beer out of a cast, the owd spuffler. I can't abide him an' never couldn't."

Gran'feyther was a milder-mannered man. "William allus bin wunnerful enviable o' me," he remarked, "but he been a poachful varmint when he could get about; there never wore a worser one."

Between the cottages of the two old men was the one in which Jim lived. He was a short, beetle-browed farm worker, and tended my garden in his spare time. Once, when I wintered abroad, I returned a few days earlier than I intended and found the beds untouched, the hedges untrimmed. Jim did not report, he just sent in a bill for three pounds for winter labour. I wrote a note to say that I could not find anything done, but if he would come up and put his back into the job, I'd pay him ten shillings for alleged work. By way of response to this challenge, he wrote me a marvellous letter in course of which he said: "For my work I cannot say but my master will give me a good charater, an' rite forward an' i will not bemean meself to work for you no more, an' i remain yours an cetrer, Mr. James Patient." I said

nothing, but one evening, a fortnight later, Jim arrived
with spade and fork.

"That don't do to let a garden goo to rewin, Master,"
he remarked, "do you gimme them ten shillin's you
promised me. Everybody gotter allow I kin do well
by a garden, if folk don't come aggravatin'." Thereafter
all went merry as a marriage bell.

Further down the road, still under the pleasant elm
tree shade, came the seventeenth century farmhouse
where "that Master Joshua" taught me to perform
acts of husbandry.

"What do you reckon I'm worth? Master Joshua,"
I asked him one day when I had hoed turnips until every
limb ached.

"I count," he replied, after a critical survey of the
rows, "you're worth a penny an hour to any farmer.
You take my advice an' goo on puttin' pieces in the
papers."

"It does pay more than a penny an hour," I admitted.

"Git over me," commented Master Joshua, "what
some folk'll do f'r a livin'. Here I am in age seventy-fower
an' never put a piece in the papers all me born days, an'
got all me teeth in me head. That's some lucky they
let ye do t' job with a pen and not with a plough—ne yet
a hoe for that matter." He never traded compliments,
though I rented his shooting and gave him my free services,
and game in due season.

On the brow of the hill from which one could see miles
of the shining estuary, two elms mingled their branches
high over the roadway. They had been planted by a
farmer to celebrate the birth of what are called twinses.
How delightfully they completed and framed the picture
until the Council—parish or rural district—decided that
they must be cut down. Only the Council knew why.
Farther along, in a house that was surrounded by trees
and boasted a fine orchard and apiary, my good friend
the Rector tended his fruit and his bees, looked after his
parishioners, and was able to give long hours to study.
He loved learning for its own sake, and was in touch
with many of the world's great old-time teachers. There

was an atmosphere of peace and goodwill in the rectory that had the quality of a visible presence.

Up and down the lane, in pursuit of occasions that were generally lawful, a few tradesmen, the carrier, the man with coal and oil, with seafaring men and summer-time tramps, passed at long intervals. The road was untended, there were no lamps, there was no water ; in return for rates I received receipts but no services.

Tilt carts, dog carts, farm carts, all these went up and down, and the farmers of those years wore whiskers and were for the most part fierce business-like men who only relaxed on market day, when they dined well at the Ordinary and declared they were ruined. The larger ones kept hunters and good port wine. The farm workers who toiled for them earned ten shillings a week, and lost time in wet weather ; they lived largely on bread, vegetables and poached rabbit. But beer was twopence a pint, fat pork fourpence a pound and tobacco fourpence an ounce, and whatever there was of shortage and suffering stayed below the surface of life. That is why the lane retained its appeal at all seasons, even on bleak winter nights when the gleam of lamp or fire touched window curtains to a note of welcome. Here was the inviolate heart of the country, and I brought to it the necessary contribution of enthusiasm and the joy of life.

II

The elms have all gone now ; here and there a bright new bungalow or villa arrests and offends the Victorian eye that can see past it to thatch and ingle nooks. But not only the trees and homes have faded into a past that few trouble to remember ; the tradesmen have gone too. You would hunt far through marshland to-day for a carrier with a tilt cart and an old horse, travelling at four miles an hour, to fetch and deliver parcels of all sizes for threepence or fourpence, earning enough to cover bare necessities for self, horse and family, and only with great difficulty putting a few shillings aside for a rainy day. The grocer's shop may bear the familiar name, but a multiple store may be the real owner, and in place of the cob and cart there will be a motor van. The old bake-oven is closed, the housewife doesn't make her own bread or jam, or cook her husband's supper, or prepare wine and cordials from the fruits and berries gathered in fields and byways. Truth to tell, the old housewife like the old tradesman has gone for all time, like the trees and period cottages, and the lane resents change; it no longer makes a rich contribution to the beauty of the world we live in, knowing perhaps that the folk who hurry up and down have eyes that see not. Was it not close to my cottage that the carrier, shining light of the Peculiar People, stopped the Vicar who was threatening to take proceedings to recover tithe on two small meadows :

" Tell me, Reveren' Spiller," he said, when he had checked his aged horse, which was so always pleased to stop, " are you of the tribe of Levi ? " " No," admitted the clergyman, a little puzzled. " Do you belong to half the tribe of Manasseh, Reveren' Spiller ? " " No, I'm afraid I don't belong to any of the tribes,"—this abruptly. " Then," declared the carrier triumphantly, " tithe ain't for the likes of you if you believe in your Bible, and if you don't you hadn't oughter be a clergyman, an' well you know it."

When what may have been the first car that ever came to the village stumbled so to speak against the garden hedge of the oldest inhabitant, he hobbled into his cottage, fetched the crooked stick that belonged to the years of his shepherding, and hit the car hard across the bonnet. " I'll learn ye, ye varmint," he cried, ignoring explanations and apologies.

The lane had never heard of motor transport; it could have learned nothing from its patrons of cars, telephone or wireless, or lighting or sanitation, of old age pensions or unemployment benefit, half holidays or a living wage. All these belonged to a future in which those who have gone had no part, and in which the lane takes no interest.

How friendly was this byway to the poachers ! In the couple of miles I knew so well there were at least a dozen turnings and half a dozen " green lanes," things apart from the road, inaccessible in winter and not easy of access after a summer shower, but often dividing arable fields and consequently a fine no-man's land and harbour for rabbits. And the rabbit, gentlest, friendliest of God's creatures, asking nothing from any farmer but sufficient food and a hole in the ground, was the worker's stand-by, often his only meat dish. There were a few hard-faced men who would prosecute a hungry toiler for taking a rabbit, and see him sent to prison in default of a fine he couldn't possibly pay, but, on the other hand, there were farmers who shut their eyes, knowing full well that they were not paying their staff a living wage.

One of these let me the shooting on his farms, and it was poached heavily; when I complained, he told me why he didn't take any action. "The men need the rabbits," he declared, "so I'm not going to interfere." "You might have told me this when you let the farm to me," I protested. "Oh, that's all right," he replied serenely, "I knew you'd find out all about it soon enough." I was too simple then to understand all that lay behind the admission, too inexperienced not to feel annoyed. Later on I became very friendly with one of the poachers.

"You're the gent what's hired th' shootin'." The speaker was a man in tatters, with an old and shabby mongrel at heel. I nodded, rather carelessly perhaps. I repeat, I was in my early twenties.

"Well, I'm the man what poaches it," he declared, frankly, "an' you can't stop me neither."

"Why not?" I demanded.

"Cause you ain't the brines," he explained. "I'll keep all on poachin' hereabouts an' there's no secret in it; I've bin an' tell't ye." So saying, he moved on. I was more interested than vexed.

"You put some water down f'r y'r partridges," he said to me later on in the summer; "don't, you'll lose 'em; most all th' springs are dry."

I think this advice, which I was quick to take, marked the beginning of a better understanding.

He lived alone in a tumble-down cottage with two rooms and a scullery, and had only his dog for friend.

One afternoon as I walked down the lane he came up to me.

"Beggin' y'r pardon, guv'nor, will ye do me a kindness?"

"What is it?" I enquired, cautiously perhaps.

"It's like this here, guv'nor. I got a summons."

"What's that for?"

"That Master Wilsmer should say I bin an' taken his rabbits. But there, he's a liar."

"You'll have to pay five shillings," I suggested, and he shook his head.

"No," he said quietly. "I bin up along o' them magistrets afore. They don't want me pennies, they got plenty o' their own, mon'srous rich most all on 'em. That's a fortnit if it ain't a month. It's Tim I'm botherin' about," and he pointed to the mongrel, "if you'd keep him for me time I'm gone—"

"But he'd fight my dogs, and I haven't a spare kennel."

"Give him a mat in yer porch. He on't touch your dogs if they don't go arter his food. He'll stay with you time I tell him to."

I couldn't refuse, at least I didn't, and Tim came to me for some weeks, for the old man's fears were well founded. Men who knew his record were on the Bench, and in those days nobody appeared to mingle much mercy with justice. The incident remains vividly in my mind, for when I took all the dogs, I had five, for their walk on the morning following his adoption, Tim came along. Suddenly he disappeared, and I decided he had gone to his master's cottage and that I must go to fetch him there lest he went hungry. But within five minutes I saw him running across the field on my right with a rabbit in his mouth. He set it down at my feet and stood still wagging his tail violently, as though asking to be praised. Luckily the meadow was part of a farm I rented for shooting.

Tim stayed with me for two or three weeks without repeating this performance; then his master returned, and it is hard to say which of them was better pleased.

Here is the odd truth. Tim and his owner passed me

after that from time to time and Tim took no notice of me. Poacher and dog have been dead more than thirty years; does anybody else remember them?

There were two notable processions along the lane, the first passed by nearly every summer, the second only once in three years; I have but to close my eyes to see both. The popular one was the fair, the procession was made up of horse-drawn vans carrying all the impedimenta of the circus as well as some stout cages holding a few unfortunate wild beasts. There might even be one or two camels in the company.

In Southern Spain, in the days when I knew the country well, the bulls would be driven along the roads in the small hours of the morning of the *corrida*, driven in the company of tame bullocks guided and controlled by *ganaderos*. One would ride ahead to warn all travellers that the bulls were coming; you could heard his cry " los toros " echoing through the night.

Here was a procedure that recalled Spain, for a cyclist would ride down the road in advance of the procession to warn farm workers not to have horses on the road; the scent of wild animals is said to throw them into a state of panic. When roundabouts and rifle gallery and refreshment stall had been set up, men would rest, and the fair would open in the early afternoon. At five o'clock the price of admission would be lowered from sixpence to threepence, and farm workers would join their families. I have seen stolid ploughmen astride the roundabout horse enjoying the music (?) of the hurdy-gurdy and eating ice creams as they went round and round.

People may wonder, as I did, how in a village where men worked for twopence or twopence-halfpenny an hour and boys for a shilling a week, money could be found to support the fair, but the reason was not far to seek. The district raised peas and strawberries, and both were picked by the veterans who no longer took regular work, by the wives of the farmhands, and by their children. For every shilling the mothers earned, the children who helped received a penny as " fairings," so that when the great day came round they might be able to enjoy all

the fun of the fair to their hearts' content. Nothing was
needed save fine weather, and when the lights went out
on the showground, sometimes the park of a rector whose
Georgian house was three miles away, there would be a
brief procession of tired happy men, women and children
going home, the fathers often carrying some youngster
already fast asleep. This was the one village festival
in three hundred and sixty-five days.

It was in connection with the fair that Gran'feyther and
the Oldest Inhabitant had their deadly quarrel. Neither
overlooked the chance of earning a little easy money,
and in the pea fields pickers were paid by results. A very
big bag, carrying twice as much or more by comparison
with those used to-day, fetched ninepence, if memory
serves. The Oldest Inhabitant was what is called " double
cunnin'." He took his time, and waited for the overseer
at the pay desk to go to dinner leaving a sturdy but stupid
lad in charge. Then with the aid of a nearby worker,
and with every appearance of fatigue, he dragged the sack
to the shed where the boy pointed to a place for it, and was
about to pay, when Gran'feyther, who had been looking
on, shouted, " Jounce 'em down boy, jounce 'em down."
The lad awakened to his duty, ran up to the sack and
shook it vigorously ; literally, as the result of a brace of
shakes, the peas fell from their high estate, leaving the
top quarter of the sack untenanted. " You mos'ly better
fill it up, Willum," he said carelessly, ignoring Gran'feyther
who stood nearby, his wrinkled face lit by smiles. The
Oldest Inhabitant's language was regrettable.

" We all gotter be honest in this here world," declared
Gran'feyther, quite unperturbed by the rich and varied
flow ; " don't, we gotter have brines." This was adding
insult to injury.

The triennial procession was brief but imposing, and
in its way sinister. The Lords of the Manor, by their
agents, came down every third year to inspect the land,
receive reports, and " proclaim " cottages that had been
lost to their owners through the damnable system of
" copyhold," now happily extinct. The Manor Lords'
representatives, as I remember them, were indescribably

old, but I was looking with the eyes of a young man.
They had an aged clerk, and drove from the station in a
yellow coach and were entertained to lunch by the squire,
and after lunch the clerk would go out to the lawn and
call in a quavering voice :

> " Oh all you who owe fealty or service to the
> Lords of the Manor, present yourselves and do
> your duty according to the Law. God save the
> Queen and the Lords of the Manor."

I cannot be sure at this distance of time that those were
the precise words, though they are perhaps near enough,
but the " Homage man " was then summoned to the
Court to tell if in the past three years anybody had
encroached upon waste land, or cut turf or altered
boundary marks, or done anything else to the detriment
of the Manor Lords. For this service rendered once
every three years, the Homage man received half-a-crown.

The Court then rose, but its work was not over. The
coach was called for again, and the aged company drove
off to neighbouring villages where certain insignificant
homes had been " proclaimed." The price of cottages
was low, with rats gnawing the boards and sparrows and
starlings breaking the thatch ; as little as forty pounds
might be the price. Farm workers struggled to buy their
homes ; they would go short of all save barest necessities
to this end, and a few succeeded, sometimes by aid of
children who had gone to the Dominions and prospered.
Then they were freed from the terror of the tied cottage, of
the home lost to them as soon as they lost their job. But
when the owner of a copyhold cottage died, the agent of the
Lords of the Manor, three wealthy corporations, could and
did demand " a fine " before they would admit the heir. If
he were comfortably circumstanced, an unusual condition,
and had a horse or cow, they could seize that ; it was a " her-
riot." Following the failure of the heir to pay his " fine,"
always a considerable one, the Lords of the Manor had to
" proclaim " the cottage three times, and as they only visited
the district once in three years their robbery might take nine
years to complete. As the rightful owner knew by now
what was coming to him, he paid no attention to repairs.

I never saw a cottage that the Lords of the Manor had restored. But derelicts multiplied, and in the end heaps of rubble marked sites of what had once been a home. I remonstrated once with the grey-bearded clerk to the Copyhold Manor Lords, and asked him if he thought that such proceedings as those he organized were a help or a hindrance to the world we live in. "Copyhold is a tenure of great antiquity," he replied, stroking his beard, "and the iconoclastic spirit that seeks to disturb established custom is greatly to be deplored. If copyhold could be abolished, tithe itself would not be safe." He knew.

III

In the days when agriculture was prosperous there would be Harvest Home suppers, but even before wheat slumped to a pound a quarter the pleasant function had passed, though it had not been forgotten. Certainly Mr. Toby Miggs who lived in the lane remembered, and came regularly to me in the early autumn for a subscription. "Master ain't none too well off nowadays," he would remind me, "so we all gotter help the harvest supper." He would come up on a Saturday night when I was entertaining friends for the week-end. "P'raps some o' y'r friends would like to spare a trifle," he would suggest delicately, and was safe to take home five or six shillings.

Then he would go to the Wheatsheaf and order the harvest supper, at which he was at once patron and sole guest. The landlady was puzzled; she asked him once why he didn't invite his wife at least, and he replied firmly that women didn't go to harvest suppers. On this great occasion he would eat a chicken and a large apple "parsty," and drink his own health in a quart or more of beer. I have been told that on that night of nights he would sleep on the couch in the kitchen, and would not take his boots off. Mrs. Miggs, bowing to the inevitable, was heard to say that a man "gotter have his own way once in a while."

People who lived round me married in the village. To go outside was to marry a "furriner." A good woman complained in great distress that her daughter—an only

child—had " gone out furrin " to choose a husband ;
a few further remarks revealed the truth that the young
man was living in the next village but one, just three
miles away. The greatest contempt was reserved for
those who went to or came from the shires, or sheers as
they were called. Essex has always stood apart, she is
not even a county of East Anglia ; the people knew it,
and took a pride in their separateness. Then, too, they
used the dialect speech with its roots in the language of
Chaucer, Wyclif and the Elizabethans, and its echoes
of the old Norman French which stands revealed in the
common speech. I have been asked for largesse, and
have been told that somebody is dolouring, or that a man
is having his bever, the eleven o'clock refreshment of the
farm worker. Dolour is based on douleur and bever on
bouvoir, and instances might be multiplied. The Great
War (as we learned to call it) killed the Essex dialect, the
young men forgot and the old folk died. Only here and
there, now and again, does it persist. Everybody who
lived in the lane used it when I was young, and there was
much in the unfamiliar words that compelled attention and
might send the listener to works of reference to find origins
that had affected marshland speech through the centuries.

Old customs persisted. Beekeepers pinned a piece of
black cloth to the hives when one of the family died ;
the looker or overseer would wait in his master's kitchen
in the good company of a round of beef and a jug of beer
to see the New Year in, and then go to the yards to wish
the stock the compliments of the season and ask them to
" make a mite o' profit for the master."

* * * * *

It is time to draw these memories to a close even to
make some apology for them, for these peaceful happenings
are not in the key of the years we live in. But it is easier
to open the floodgates of memory than it is to shut them
again, while a host of uneventful happenings strive to
gain their brief moment of renewed life. My lane must
be as a thousand others were, even though it was more
beautiful than most, and the folk living there, many as

much at home on the water as on the land, may have been specially interesting. Though London was little more than fifty miles away and its outposts were thrusting far into rural Essex, they had not discovered marshland. To-day there are changes, ugly and plentiful, and one must seek memory's aid to see the lane as it was, a part of rural England, peaceful and inviolate.

At the same time, let us admit that the external beauty covered much ugliness. Life was intolerably harsh for the farm worker and his family, whose status was little better than that of serfs. All the social amenities enjoyed to-day were unheard of, and the sick were often entrusted to the care of " wise men " and " wise women," who treated all ailments with the same concoction of herbs and killed many more than they cured. Without sickness benefit, with a poor law relief that was an insult to poverty, with no old age pension, no maternity grant, the lot of the poor was pitiable and unpitied, their courage and good spirits past all praise.

Through the seven months of the marshland winter the lane saw unhappiness, privation and suffering ; through late spring, summer and early autumn the land radiated happiness, while the extra money from pea fields, straw-berry grounds and harvest lightened the burden of life, if only for a little while.

Yes, the beauty of the lane has gone, and the men and women who gave it individuality have followed the immemorial elms and the period cottages, but the birds still sing and flowers fill the hedgerows, and many harsh and intolerable conditions have followed those who suffered from them into the unknown, never to return. Life is easier, kinder, more fun—and not so good to look upon from the point of view of the man who still expects a pageant, because this was what he saw with eyes that were untrained to take in all the scene and its underlying significance.

Moreover, when you are young and are living in your own cottage, entertaining friends as carefree as yourself, having shooting rights over a lot of land and breathing the vital air that comes across the North Sea, ugliness passes unheeded.

BACK TO EARTH

By PETER HOWARD

THE oldest roads in the world sidle through spinneys and copses. They slink along the headlands of the arable land between the brow of the ditch and the springing corn. They creep silently and secretly close to the hedges and beneath the tangled trees.

Sometimes these age-old thoroughfares find their way at last on to the ordnance map, with a thin dotted line to mark their track. Mostly they remain unknown except to those who have made them, the generations of yeomen and farm-hands, poachers, trappers and sweethearts who, century upon century, have trodden them out with the eternal thud, thud, thud of agricultural boots against the soil.

Men live. Men die. But the sounds of the travellers along those earthen highways remain the same for ever—the quick scuffle of workmen cutting to their labours across the fields in the dark before an icy Winter dawn, the slow and weary clump of the homecomers, pausing under the lee of the old oak as their fathers and grandfathers and great-grandfathers did before them, for a moment's muttered conversation before they break up and go their ways to the evening meal.

" Looks like we'll have a frost to-night."

" Do, it'll only be a wind frost then, bor."

" I doubt we'll get no frosts this moon, not to say *frosts*."

So they part with a chorus of " Good-nights." A muttered laugh or a whistled tune with a snatch of distant words is thrown backwards towards the branches of the oak through the mounting dusk. The old tree stirs and shudders. It would be on the move like a proud ship before the evening breeze were it not for its deep anchorage in the soil.

The ancient hedge and highway is left alone to add another to its burden of ten thousand, thousand nights.

It is left alone for the sweethearts first and later for the poachers, and finally for the hares and foxes, the rabbits and moles and little bright-eyed creatures who scurry their way across it, each intent on his own small business of life and love, death and survival, in those still silent hours of blackness before another dawn.

*　　*　　*　　*　　*

My forebears were fenmen. For generations they drove their ploughs through the black earth of the East Anglian fens, that part of England which gave Cromwell his Ironsides, where Nelson lived his boyhood, and whence the Pilgrim Fathers gathered before their voyage to found a new world.

But I was born a townsman. I grew up in the bustle and clamour and smell of cities, a Londoner by adoption, a brother of the Black Craft, pushing a pen in Fleet Street by the Thames.

My pen had a nib of gold. I pushed it as doggedly and continuously as my ancestors pushed their ploughs in East Anglia, and it earned me a salary larger than that of some Cabinet Ministers.

I knew something of the theory of farming, but nothing of the practice of it. I used to write many leading articles telling the Government how to treat the farmers and the farmers how to treat the land. Neither took my advice, and I am bound to tell you this did nothing to lower my opinion of their good sense or ability.

In the corner of my mind was a picture of myself at the age of fifty, with enough money to retire to the country and farm the earth. I had an instinct which said that, if we wished to build a nation with a sound heart, someday we should have to put back into the land the money which for years we had drained away from the country to the cities.

So I imagined myself, a gaitered and distinguished-looking gentleman, with greying hair, inspecting cornfields which undulated hazily into the distance or sniffing the tobacco scent of the hay in June as my men loaded the tumbrils, or walking the roots in Autumn with friends and a gun, as hare and partridge and pheasant filled the bag.

This was a beautiful dream. Like most dreams, it had little contact with reality. For in those days I knew nothing of the endless battle with the earth, the struggle against weeds and wet, pests and weather, the blisters, cold and exhaustion, the cost and sweat of tillages, the planning and perils and disappointments before any one crop is harvested from the soil.

I was simply a townsman who loved the country so long as he did not have to live there—who was enthusiastic about short week-ends in old cottages, so long as these had been equipped with central heating, hot water, first-rate cooking and every other modern comfort.

One day, during such a week-end, a friend told me that two and a half miles away a farm was for sale. Together we went to look at it.

Farms are sold at so many pounds per acre, with the farmhouse and buildings all included in that price. Your true fenman farmer, with his roots in the earth, will sometimes buy a farm without inspecting the farmhouse at all. That, for him, is the least important part of the bargain. If the land is well-drained, the hedges down, the fields clean and the soil in good heart, it is enough for him. He makes his bid for the property.

But when I went with my friend to look at the farm for sale, I thought of more than these things.

The hedges of the property grew twenty feet and more into the air, thick in proportion.

But the old farmhouse had a vast Elizabethan chimney, and as you peered upward from the bricked kitchen floor you could see sooted hooks where for centuries the hams had smoked, and above them crannies filled with swallows' nests, and at the top a bright square of sky with clouds running across it.

I pictured myself and my family around that fireplace at night-time when the day's toil was done, with home-grown logs, vast and dry as tinder, roaring upwards towards the stars.

The land was sour and foul, badly drained in many places.

But I saw the huge tithe barn arching like a cathedral into the gloom of the thatch dome, with oak beams which had hung there for four hundred years, and before that had weathered the storms and frosts of five hundred Winters in their lifetime as trees.

I had a vision of my children playing hide-and-seek among bulging sacks, and vast pyramids of golden corn glowing in the dark corners of the barn and illuminating them.

For years little had been done to the farm, which was near derelict, and the land was in poor heart. But there were the relics of nobility in the shape and feel of the property, a sense about it that it had seen days which were great ones, and that master-crops had once been grown there, the topic and admiration of the countryside.

Down by the boundary we came upon an old bent man with a wrinkled, walnut countenance, who leant on a broken gate, his eyes hazy with wisdom and memory. " Do you know this farm ? " I asked him.

Before answering he considered me in the slow, contemplative fashion which comes to those who have spent a lifetime dependent on their own labours and God's providence. Then he said, " Should do, master, seeing I worked there more than fifty year. There ain't many yards of that land I haven't dropped me sweat upon, I doubt."

" What sort of a place is it ? " I asked him. " Oh, the old farm is right enough if it's done right," he told me, without a tone either of affection or of hatred for the place. " But it's been let go. It'd take a few years to get it round now, I reckon." Then he said, " I remember forty year back it were the best farm hereabouts. Mr. Bardolph had it then, a rare old dealer he were. I've seen he with as many as eighty Suffolk horses in them midders, and all of 'em agone the week after. Cleared right out of them, he would. But he did the place well—there was always a couple or three yards of bullocks on the go, and if he'd seen the straw sent off the land that's been sold the last few years from here, why it would have druv he half crazy. We never grew less nor twelve coomb an acre of wheat and fourteen or fifteen coomb an acre of barley in them days—and thistles and docks, why the old place is half poisoned with 'em now. But Mr. Bardolph, he used to take his friends a walk round the farm of a Sunday afternoon, and he'd offer a bob for every thistle or dock, and he didn't have to pay out much neither, I can tell ye."

I thanked the old man for all his news. He looked at me and said, " Do ye reckon on buying the place, master ? "

" That depends on the price," I said. " Oh, it'll go cheap enough now, or should do," he answered. " Well, ye could travel further and do worse. Some of them fields are funny old customers to plough, though, no mistake. But good luck, master, and don't ye let they *do* ye."

So we parted from the old man, who now lies under the earth to which he gave his life. As we walked away from that derelict, delightful farm, my heart was set on owning it. There was a longing in me to stand with both feet on a bit of English earth, to look at the fields and hedges and crops and cattle around me and to say to the world, " This is mine."

I was groping with my heart for something more permanent in life than the shifting scene of salaries, bonuses and the sack which is Fleet Street.

A few days later I told Doe, my wife, " Well, it is ours. We are farmers now."

" I suppose you are quite sure it isn't a mad thing to do ? " Doe asked me.

I became angry when she said this. For I half thought it *was* a mad thing to do. I can bear ill-founded criticism of myself better than criticism founded in truth. If I find myself tempted to prickle with rage at something which is said to me about myself, I know that what has been said is near the mark.

However, any uneasy feelings I had about the wisdom of buying a derelict farm were covered by the joy of possession and the knowledge that my salary was still rolling in from Fleet Street, adequate to meet any financial emergency.

* * * * *

We guard the soil. On silent Winter nights
When frost has steeled the furrows, and the ponds
Are armoured shields against the invading moon,

D

We hear the earth soft-breathing.   Understand
Earth is no dead, unfeeling bulk of clay
But animate strength, with heart and lungs and limbs
Wounded by greed, yet sensitive to care.
Earth is God's living workman.   Age by age
Abundantly it turns death into life.
Wet mulched manures, the dry composted heaps
Of wood-ash, grass, and lime : decaying straw,
The bones and flesh of beasts, the blood of men—
All touch the earth, and change and stir and live.
No particle of food in all the world,
Is fit for men until it has endured
The alchemy and potence of the soil.
All dead things come to life within the earth
Slowly, inevitably.   But man desires
The quick return, cash-cropping, money yields.
He will not wait for years while the manures
Moulder and break and form a tilth of soil
With heart and muscle, rich and purposeful.
While in his yards slow bullocks tread the straw
And crunch the beans and sweat and breathe and sleep.
They plunge and rustle all the Winter through
Knee deep in straw, while underneath their feet
The hot, moist dungle rises—till they stride
Over the gates that penned them in as calves,
And leave behind a legacy of life
To kernel corn and swell globed golden roots
Out of the land in harvests yet unsown.

Man gets nothing from the earth except what he puts
back into it.

We have learned on our farm that the land feeds the
people when the people feed the land.   Also that the soil
is a good servant but a savage master.   Once it is allowed
its liberty, and the weeds recapture the fields and the
hedges infiltrate the headlands, it becomes as hard to bring
land back to fruitful service as to tame a jungle beast.

I planned to spend money freely in hedging, ditching,
draining and manuring.   But suddenly a crisis in my affairs
arose.   I started to write a book* giving the facts and telling

*"Innocent Men" (Heinemann 2/6)

the truth about a subject which had been misrepresented in the newspapers. I was then informed that I could write a book on anything else I liked, except this particular matter.

I thought things over carefully. Self-interest urged me to drop the book and continue my Fleet Street progress. But there was that in me which said that truth and fair play and justice were in the long run more important than the fate of one journalist, even a journalist so important to myself as me.

So I left Fleet Street.

As I sat in the corner of my third-class carriage travelling towards East Anglia, where Doe and our three children already had gone, I knew the emotions of excitement and fear.

I was frightened because my income had vanished and I had no cash to spare. It was do or die. My farming friends had told me it must be at least three years before the derelict land could stop losing money.

I was excited because I was face to face with the oldest problem of mankind—how to wrest food from the unyielding soil. I was a city man with soft hands, small knowledge and an ignorant enthusiasm, turning back to the land. I felt the zest of one who is about to put to the issue something which for a long time he has considered—whether it is possible for unskilled city dwellers to go back to earth.

I knew that if I could do it, anybody could.

I had a sense of adventure almost as if I were landing with my family on some unknown continent and settling there to make a home.

I knew that our experience as a family could pioneer the path for many, if we succeeded—for in the years ahead men from the Forces and from the cities, faced with the problems of the post-war world, would turn back to Britain's idle acres in search of bread if someone could lead the way there.

That evening in our farmhouse, with the children put to bed upstairs in a bare room with oak beams, Doe and I camped in the unfurnished kitchen, cooking stew on a Primus stove.

In the old Fleet Street days (only a week before, already remote in our hearts), we often dined at the Savoy at midnight amid the lights and perfume, the paint and wine and music of a rich and artificial age.

Now as we spooned stew into our mouths, with an oil lamp stuck on a deal table as our companion, an inquisitive mouse stuck his nose through a cranny in the ancient farmhouse wall and peeped at us. I hit at him with a table spoon and missed.

We laughed together, Doe and I, and moved upstairs, gazing down by the light of the lamp on our three children drawing their soft, deep breaths in sleep. What would they say of the decision we had taken when they were old enough to understand it ?

We felt a tug of fear at the heart and a throb of resolve also. Before we went to bed that first night in our new home we knelt and prayed to God for strength and courage.

This was something we had lost the way of doing in our years in Fleet Street.

*   *   *   *   *

Break a field and make a man. That is what countrymen said in days of old. They knew what they were saying. Anyone who has grappled with the wild land, broken its spirit and made a servant of it, has experienced an education better than any the universities can offer.

The battle with the soil is unending. It continues every day, seven days a week, Winter, Spring, Autumn and Summer, whether the outer world is at peace or at war. The same day that a husbandman ceases to exert his strength and skill against the earth, the earth begins its swift and silent retreat back to the jungle.

Our first year on the farm we left the hedges to look after themselves. Day after day we sat upon the tractors ploughing, crooming and cultivating land, some of which had been the undisturbed home of ragwort, dock and thistle for over twenty years.

The hedges had crept out on to the land ten and fifteen yards in some places.

We skirted them and sat doggedly on our tractors, from dawn till dusk, cranking the heavy engines with cracked and blistered hands as the first glimmers of light shone through the darkness, switching from petrol to oil as the engine grew hot after a few minutes' work, and chugging steadily through the day, our bodies aching with fumes and vibration, chilled by the wind and mizzle of rain which blows in from the North Sea, but cheered by the even furrows of good earth laid in neat rows behind us, where wilderness had been before. At the end of each day, the ploughshares came out of the clay like smooth and burnished swords. They had a slight, comforting warmth from the friction of their passage through the cold, wet earth.

In the evenings we worked to restore the old glory of the farmhouse. Sixteen layers of bright wallpaper were stripped off one room before we came to what lay beneath—a copy of a newspaper dated 1832, with an account of how a bull ran amok at Bury St. Edmunds and killed a dog before it was mastered, and the iron-hard beauty of the oak beams with the marks of the mattock still upon them.

We uncovered an ancient chimney-piece, and found in the corner of it the sign of the master builder which he had scratched with compasses on finishing the job centuries ago.

Doe and I had to set our hands to tasks we never had done before. Our farm buildings were falling to pieces.

We planned and built our first new building, marking and measuring its foundation with sticks and string on the soaking meadow grass one dark November morning. We sunk the corner posts, sloped the roof, sawed the beams and weatherboarding, our unaccustomed hands and minds being perplexed and bruised at almost every small operation.

How that building rose at all, in view of what I have learned since, I cannot think. But it still stands. Pigs, horses, and many other live and dead stock have found their home in one of its four stalls.

We made so many mistakes, Doe and I. But we learned from each one of them.

The foundation of the tithe barn, laid by skilful hands now four hundred years in their graves, had sagged, and the whole structure was in danger. We dug a trench, and built a light wooden framework enclosing the old foundations and the thick-set oaken beams which once had rested on them, but now gaped several inches apart. Then we mixed sand and cement, made concrete and poured it into our wooden framework out of buckets, so that the beams and foundation were knit and buttressed into a solid whole.

Our yards began to fill with stock. With the buying of stock we also bought experience. We quickly learned the bitter lesson of the handsome cow, with shiny hide and swelling udders, which proudly faces the dealers and the auctioneers at the local market. You take it home—and a few days later discover why such a fine-looking animal was for sale. The best beasts do not find their way to the ring.

We planned to increase our herd of cows, so they should fertilize the hungry fields, which had smelt little muck for a decade and were hilly and awkward to plough.

Cows have the golden hoof. They and their children are becoming the walking muckcarts of our farm. The hoof of sound stock, and the eye and sweat of the farmer on every inch of every field—these things are the surety and safeguard of success in any farming venture.

We made an onslaught upon the rabbits. In our first twelve months on the farm we killed over a thousand of them. For years they had bred and burrowed around our headlands, eating acres of corn down to the ground, leaving the earth sour and foul behind them. We killed them with sticks and dogs as they darted for safety from the narrowing strips of corn at harvest time. Later we hunted them with spades, nets, guns and ferrets from the first foggy days of early November, when we stood shivering with the cold under the dripping hedges waiting for the pests to bolt, to the later days of March when we sat down coatless to eat our nineses, our faces in the sunshine and our feet dipped in the young, green corn.

We attacked the hedges. It took me and one of my men two hours of ceaseless toil to cut through and open

up one gateway which the blackthorn and nut and crab
had overgrown. On the coldest days of Winter, days
when the whole earth was gripped by the iron hands of
the frost, when you could sometimes hear deep down
beneath you a sound like a groan as some rock cracked
under the probe and wrench and icy leverage of Winter's
force, we worked, a team of us, until the sweat washed
channels down the dirt on our faces.

We chopped and hacked and sawed down the jungle
growth of a quarter of a century. We burned it up
behind us, and the charcoal dust from the fires stuck
in the sweat on our brows and hands and made us look
like blackamoors amid the snows of Winter.

> Scan the wild hedges, how they straggle high,
> Thorn-taloned, stiff-necked barriers.   Underneath
> Octopus rootlets tentacle the land
> And suck and scar its bounty.   While above
> The jungle foliage screens both wind and sun,
> So headland corn is peaked and green and stunt,
> Half-ripened and unkernelled.   Hedges too
> Cottage the vermin which by night and day
> Gorge and destroy—while Old Man's Beard crawls
>   forth
> Like Sin, among the beans, to strain and twist,
> To strangle and divide.   For many years
> No hand has hacked the hedges on our Hill.
> For " Hedging does not pay."   Long hours of toil
> Without the immediate recompense in cash—
> That is the stewardship the earth demands
> And lacking it, has ailed.   So now we cleave
> Our hedges, black as Hell and barbed as Hate,
> With hook and axe and bill.

Steam engines came and broke up with deep cultivations
the hard pan of clay, which years of shallow ploughing
to the same depth had left beneath the surface of many
of our fields.

We set about the land with stubborn ferocity, for we
felt in our bones and heart that if we did not beat it, it
would beat us. At times we came near to despair, with
our ignorance and our unaccustomed city muscles which

took months to attune to the strength and cunning of the soil.

It is in the nature of a townsman to look for quick results and swift returns. The soil does not offer these things. It may take four or five years' skilful and costly husbandry to bring virtue back to a field which has lost strength.

So Doe and I had to conquer our early impatience. We set ourselves to the long-term exercise of brain and muscle and humility which is the education the soil offers to all who serve it with their hands and hearts.

* * * * *

Townsmen who go back to earth are at first helpless creatures. They do not know the smell of the dawn or the rule of the moon upon the weather.

They can do for themselves none of the things which countryfolk learn as soon as they walk. The feeding of stock, the hoeing of roots, the harnessing of horses, the planting of seed, the loading of straw into a cart and the driving of it through a gate without knocking down the post—all these things they must learn.

Every simple and small task in the country needs skill, as I found when I came to try them.

Learning is sometimes a painful business which makes a man look a fool. Countryfolk are themselves by nature sensitive, they are terrified of appearing foolish and become angry when in danger of it. This makes them enjoy laughter all the more when somebody else makes a fool of himself.

Countryfolk watch you, when first you come to live among them. If you pretend to know things you do not know, if you get angry when folk laugh at your early mistakes and incompetence, countryfolk will offer you politeness but not friendship. You will remain a stranger.

If you are humble enough to learn everything, even carrying a forkful of straw, from the beginning (and there is a right and wrong way of doing this as there is of doing everything else in the world), if you are able to join good-humouredly in the laugh against yourself, countrypeople take you to their hearts. They will do anything to help you.

When first I moved to East Anglia people laughed at my accent and the way I talked. I only understood half they said to me, and was tempted to laugh at their accent too. But on reflection, the simpler and wiser course seemed to be to learn the meaning of words like " meesen " (mice), " nasen " (nests), " four-a-lete " (cross-roads), " stingy " (bad-tempered), and dozens more, which sprinkled every conversation and baffled me. Also to teach myself to speak in the simple terms and tones which my new neighbours understood.

The countryfolk laughed at some of the orders I gave my men. In early days, because I knew no better, sometimes I used to tell them to plough when the weather had made the land unfit to plough, or order them to roll the young corn when it would have harmed the crops for them to do it.

They would look at each other when these orders were given, but were too polite to make any reply. They would go off to the fields, and return to me after half an hour or so with the comment, " Can't work it to-day, Master," usually making some suggestion of their own about what they should do. It always was a good suggestion.

I was tempted to get annoyed at this. I felt that they were in some way making a fool of me, their boss. But presently I realized that if I was a fool, I was a self-made one, and one morning I asked the men to tell me if an order which I gave them was impractical.

From that moment they offered me loyalty and friendship. Working with them I learned the elements of husbandry, and they came to respect my judgment in many things as I recognized the value of their inherent instinct and skill for the soil.

No one is more delightful a companion than an East Anglian craftsman if you have his confidence. Their jokes and words are a delight. The other day, as I and one of my men were drilling corn together, an old Suffolk mare passed slowly by on the road. " She needs to move a bit quicker than that," I said. Sam replied, " Nor she won't till she's inside a greyhound."

My cowman refused one of Lord Woolton's agricultural

pies with the comment, " Cor, I wouldna eat one of they.
Last time I et one of they I found an old rat's claw inside
he." I may add, in case Lord Woolton is downcast by
this verdict, that for over a year we have been eating his
pies in my farmhouse at least once a week, and have found
many good things inside them, but never a rat's claw.

One of my London friends, who visited us a day or so
ago, was surprised when within a few minutes of arrival
at the farm he was asked by a farm boy how tall he was.
The boy explained that he had a bet on about this subject.
The boy told me afterwards, " That gentleman is surely
master tall, Sir. I never seed one as tall as he afore. Why,
he'd make a couple of errand-boys if you cut he in two."

When this season my field of peas grew fast, at a time
when much other farm work was on hand, Sam's comment
to me about them was, " They'll be ready for we, afore
we'm ready for they, I doubt."

At 5.45 a.m. on the day when a bomb fell in one of
my ditches, I found a crowd inspecting the crater before
breakfast and their morning work. An acre or two of
oats had been blasted by the explosion. My horseman
used these words to describe the event to me. " It has
boomped in the ditch, Sir. It nipped off them oats like
they'd been nibbled by old rabbits." Then, after a pause
for thought, " It were worse nor rabbits, I doubt."

No man could wish for better comrades and friends
than the men who to-day work the land with Doe and
me. They have the long-range perspective which comes
to those who know you can neither rule nor hurry the
ageless processes of nature.

They have the true loyalty which allows them to be
honest and blunt, even if at first you may not like it.

They know from daily renewed experience that when
man has done all he can for the land, the rest depends
on God. So many of them have implanted in them a
Christian faith, that sturdy taproot of character which
nourished our greatness as a nation.

*   *   *   *   *

We wrestled and fought this derelict farmland together,
my men and I. When I bought it, the farm was graded

"C." That is the lowest grade of farm in my neighbourhood, the grade at which farms are taken away from farmers and farmed in the national interest by the War Executive Committee.

But as I was a new man come in, they gave me a chance. They waited to see what I could do.

We ploughed and cultivated and croomed. We harrowed and rolled and hoed. We worked at the hedges with sweating bodies and bleeding hands.

In the wet Autumn weather we drilled our wheat, the horses struggling through the heavy loam with mud caked to the barrel of their chests, their breath jutting out before them like twin trumpets. When the rain fell, we struggled on, soaked through, man and beast together, and consoled ourselves with the old Suffolk saying, " Sow in a flood, reap in a wood "—which means that wheat often grows thick as a forest when it is sown with the rain pouring down.

Only one seed in four of those we drill will reach maturity if the old-time song is true. Farmers sang it as they broadcast their seed :

> " One for the rook,
> One for the crow,
> One to rot,
> And one to grow."

But the wheat which does win through to growth is one of the toughest plants in the world. You can harrow it this way and that, roll it with ton-rollers, trample it with horses, feed sheep on it if it is winterproud, and still there is a harvest.

One small seed of wheat "tillers" and throws forth perhaps eight stalks of corn, and each of them will tower three feet into the air. The seed of wheat buried in the earth in October, dies there, and from its dying throws forth by the following August blades and ears many thousand times its own size.

Each little grain, if you look closely, has the shape and features of a tiny face upon it. The face gazes forth from each grain of wheat as though enfolded and covered by swaddling clothes. Some old countrymen believe it is the face of the Christ child, marked on the grain which, by an annual miracle, gives all mankind his daily bread.

Slowly, as a result of our labours, the farm began to mend.

We grew ten sacks of corn per acre where six had grown before. Next year the figure crept to twelve.

By careful and continuous hand cultivation through the Summer we produced three times as many mangolds off four acres of land as we had lifted off ten acres the season before.

In Autumn the huge roots thudded into the bottom of the tumbrils with a sound like thunder, and the hearts of myself and my men rose as we felt the unyielding earth begin to budge before our labours.

Throughout the Winter we sent over forty gallons of milk daily off the farm, where no cow moved or snored or chewed before we came there.

From the worst field on the farm (" Ye won't grow nowt there, mister, not nohow, I reaken ") we cropped sixteen sacks an acre of oats.

One day some gentlemen drove up to our farmhouse door in a car. They were members of the War Executive Committee, and had come to inspect our land. They coupled friendship with efficiency. They gave me advice which has proved invaluable. From the first day until now their help in our enterprise has been constant and worthy of gratitude. We walked together from field to field in silence. Sometimes they asked me questions about the cropping of the fields and made notes in a little book. Then they shook my hand and departed.

A month later, I received the following letter :

DEFENCE REGULATIONS, 1939.

Dear Sir,

The Executive Committee, on the advice of the appropriate District Committee, are very pleased to raise the classification of your farm to " A," and to express their appreciation of your efforts in bringing about this result.

Yours faithfully,

(Signed)

Executive Officer.

Grade " A " is the highest grade obtainable in this district. Doe and I looked at each other across the table. Well, we had done it. We knew that whatever became of us in the future, whether we lived on the land or in the cities, rich or poor, sick or well, things would never be quite the same again for us.

To be at grips with the earth, to bleed and sweat and be bruised in the battle with it, is an age-old experience which educates men and leaves them different. Their sense of true values alters and is renewed. They look at things, and men too, from a fresh angle. They do not give up so easily and they are never so readily fooled. They have something unbreakable in the heart of them, born in the hope of inevitable harvest after the months of mud and cold.

To such men earth can become a lover, a servant, a friend, the spirit of deep and quiet and everlasting things.

So Doe and I looked at each other across our farmhouse table. From outside came the shrill barking of pigs as some of their comrades were loaded into a lorry for market. Also the cries and laughter of our children as they helped drive the cows to milk.

We heard the wind rustle the lime trees and a shaft of sunshine smote the wall, now neatly plastered, through which an inquisitive mouse had stuck his nose on our first evening in the farm.

I got up and kissed Doe. Then I moved out of the back door to my work, putting on a cap as I went. Grade " A " or not, so much still remained to be done.

This piece of earth had wrestled with many generations before I came on the scene, and would strive with many more after I had departed. It knew no rest in its ceaseless bounty of the centuries—and those who serve it cannot afford to pause in their toil.

* * * * *

What do we want from the earth ? What is its future to be ? So many farmers and countrymen cynically accept the belief that as soon as the dangers of war are lifted from us, British agriculture will once more be allowed to decay and decline.

Most of our population live in cities. The city vote governs the nation. City folk, as a rule, do not care for the land.

The land is something more than a business. It is a way of life.

Some farmers treat the earth as a kind of cash register. They bang and bully and beat it, they turn it upside down and shake it until the last penny has dropped out of it, and then leave it sucked and dispoiled and move on to the next farm. These men have the same approach to the earth as many city dwellers—that it must be judged according to the interest on invested capital which it returns.

In old days men used to say, " Live as though you would die to-night. Farm as though you would live for ever." By it they meant that character was as important as cash, and that the way to farm land was to look after it and build into it, instead of thinking of it constantly in terms of how much in cash could be got out of it.

Britain's land is the one inexhaustible national asset we possess. Nothing can waste or destroy or touch it except ourselves. Its hope for the future is a return to the old conception of stewardship where all men believe that if God gives something to them, He means it to be used, not wasted.

Did God give Britons their soil, the finest in all the world, to use and develop or to waste if that suits the pockets of the financiers ? Britain's growing arable acreage could provide life-work for hundreds of thousands of families, and a life-work calling for all that the best of work does offer—craftsmanship, character and courage.

We could and should become a healthier nation and recapture the joy and soundness of heart which made other nations call us " Merrie England " in the days before cinemas, central heating and garden suburbs were created to keep us happy.

Land draws the best out of those who offer their best to it. It is a factory of character—and character is the framework of a nation.

If we are to have the better world we all long for, we shall get it by becoming better people. No other way. It is conceivable that on the land, in the fields and villages of Britain, a new spirit can be born to fill our island with peace and laughter and love one for another.

Some land girls work for me and Doe. They live in the farmhouse with us. Until war broke out, all of them lived in cities. They were typists, milliners or clerks. This is the charter for our farm, which they wrote together after they had worked for some months on the land :

FARM CHARTER

" God gave us this land.

" It had been pillaged by man's greed. The soil was starved and the buildings were neglected.

" We pledge ourselves to hand on to the future better than we have received from the past. It is our purpose to make this place perfect.

" We neither expect ease nor ask for it. We look to each hardship as an opportunity and each new job as an adventure.

" Perfect work in every last detail is our aim. When we have hoed a field, no weed shall be left upon it. Every tool after a task is done shall be put back in its proper place. We will keep each stall and sty so clean that no disease may spread or spring among our animals.

" The heart of the farm is the family. Love and loyalty to each other are the cement which unites us.

" We plan to create in our family a part of the new Britain. We shall drive out of our family life everything wise men hate in the old Great Britain. We shall bring to birth those things all men long for in the new and greater Britain that is to be.

" This shall be a family where discipline replaces drift—a family without moods. No demand for place, privilege or position shall deaden, dull or drive us.

" We seek no profit for ourselves from the land. We hold all things in common and in trust from God.

" This family has no limit. Everyone who comes here, whether for a day or a year, is part of it. It is a family which does not depend on names or riches, class or age.

" We are out to rebuild men as well as to feed them. We dedicate ourselves to sacrificial God-controlled living which alone can create a better world. We live not for to-day and for ourselves but for the future and for others."

So the spirit of this charter can spread through our nation, starting with me and you. If we can change

from the spirit of " What do I get out of my country ? "
to " What can I give my country ? " we may see our
children grow up in that age we longed for but never
achieved.

Now, under God, we guardians of the soil
Dedicate all we have in toil and prayer,
Not for the swift return in cash and kind,
But recreating craft in husbandry,
And stewardship and quiet sufficiency.
So both our cottages and farms shall know
The multitudinous fruitage of the soil.
The barns shall sag and tremble with the corn
Beam-high, rich pyramids of warmth and gold.
Broad stallions, thunderous hooved, shall pace the
    earth
And fertilize the pastures.   While the cows
Wax fat and richly yield in calf and cream.
Huge hogs shall grunt and snore away their time.
While bees garner the honey murmurously,
We, stewards of the Hill, plan under God
To shape this farm to perfect purposes,
Faithful in every detail, so to mould
This message to the nation and the world.

THE CALL OF THE LAND

THE SPIRIT OF THE NEW AGRICULTURAL PIONEERS

Photographs taken on the Suffolk Farm of the Author of " Back to Earth "
by RICHARD N. HAILE, F.I.B.P., F.R.P.S., *former President Institute of British Photographers*

HILL FARM
Four hundred years ago it was built. Three years ago it was derelict.

The farmer and his wif
who came to the derelic
farm. They are Pete
Howard, former Englan
Rugby Captain, then poli
tical columnist with th
Beaverbrook newspapers
and his wife, Doë Metaxa
the Wimbledon tennis sta

The beams of the house and barn were timbers of some stout ship
that sailed the Spanish Main in the days of Drake and Raleigh.

The village is over two miles away. Pony and trap
provide transport for the farmer and his family.

Harvest time in Constable's county. The road leads uphill to the farmhouse.

Summer morning. A miner's son from the Welsh Valleys is getting the pony ready for the day.

Three cats to a hundred acres is the Suffolk way. Hill Farm is 264 acres and has more than its ration of cats. They are mighty hunters. They keep themselves on rats, and the rabbits they catch are even taken home by the farm men for the family pie.

Beaverbrook has a will of his own. This pedigree Friesian
bull is the future father of the Brentleigh herd.

Snowball, the shorthorn bull, is enticed to show
his head above the half-door.

Stan has been milking cows since he was eight, so he can " larn 'em ". If the cow-house walls aren't scrubbed every day you hear from Stan.

First the cows must be milked by the machines which Stan is carrying, above. Then, below, their udders must be stripped by hand.

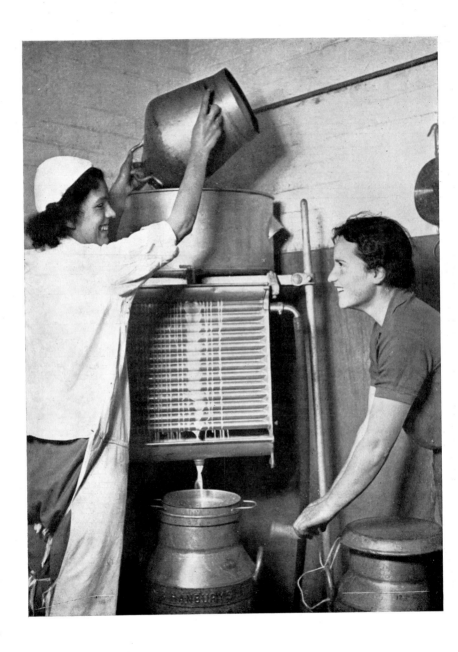

Mary, ex-dressmaker from Manchester, and Phoebe a Bournemouth solicitor's daughter, working together in the cowshed.

Steady care means sound stock—" We will keep each stall and sty so clean that no disease may spread or spring among our animals," says the farm's charter (p. 63).

The farmer with Tom the tractor driver. Tom is Suffolk born and bred.

Right.
Dinner is served !

Bottom right.
Spring work. A wide harrow drawn at a steady pace soon covers a lot of ground.

Below.
Fred the foreman. He knows the secret of every job on the land.

Above.   Margaret, ex-typist, feeds the pigs.   In Suffolk they say, " Always take a bucket in one hand and a stick in the other when feeding pigs.   If you have to leave one behind, leave the bucket."
Below.   Silhouettes against the morning sky.   A goat is led to her tethering post.

A land girl. Lucy is one of the authors of the " Farm Charter." She was previously employed by a London store.

He spent his holidays harvesting. Head boy of a public school, then at Oxford, he later goes overseas with the R.A.F.

" The fields are ripe unto harvest."

All is safely gathered in. Big, bulky shapes, yield of the
year's work, fill the rickyard.

Hill Farm Harvest Home, 1942

The farmer and his wife, and children, the landgirls, the farm men and their families, the thatcher, the blacksmith, the local builder and his wife, a company of seventy, sit down to eat together and to thank God for the harvest and the new spirit that is coming to the land. They celebrate also the raising of the farm to the top " A " category of excellence, three years after the farmer had bought it as derelict.

A PIECE OF OLD SURREY

By H. J. Massingham

Even Surrey is ancient; it was not laid out in convenient proximity to the Great Wen to serve as a dormitory or week-end resort for the umbrella and the black coat. Even Surrey was once part of an England that, like the universe, was occupied by constellations of solar systems, each with its sun or market town ringed about by planetary villages in magnetic relation to it by means of surplus commodities. It was more ancient even than what we call the " Dark Ages," the ages, that is to say, of the Craft Guilds and the Cathedrals. It is even more archaic than the valley between Abinger Hammer and Gomshall which was carved out by a stream you can step over, a stream that is no more than the affluent of a tributary of the Wey, but was once broad and turbulent enough to take up the whole valley for its bed. Perhaps there was still a Surrey even before that, possessing a number of distinguishing signs and identifications whereby what we mean by Surrey was different from what we mean by Sussex or Middlesex.

Only in recent years has that self-identity been compromised and overlaid; it was maintained through more æons than we can be aware of. Many flint arrow-heads and scrapers have been found in this flat valley and on the chalk Downs above where lies " The Tote," from which have been dug urn fragments—perhaps it was once an urn-field of the Iron Age. The word tote or toot simply means pry or peer, and was more often than not the site of a prehistoric burial ground from which the fairies peeped when the coast was clear. On these Downs, and they are sizeable Downs, not much lower of elevation in parts than Gilbert White's " chain of majestic mountains " to the south-east, the Pilgrim's Way and the Harroway, or Hoarway, run parallel to one another, the first not above four hundred feet, the other a kind of Ridge Way and so the older. This same parallelism of

F

THE SILENT POOL

ancient ways occurs again in Berkshire, where the Icknield Way travels west just above the line of springs but several hundred feet below the truly majestic Ridge Way that links Wayland's Smithy with the Blowing Stone, both of them belonging to the first megalithic period of about 1800 B.C. The same father and daughter Ways swing along from Butser to Beachy Head and even over the Chilterns where, in spite of them being once densely forested and now suburbanized, the old roads were, as we say in our jargon, " in triplicate," and are still to be traced. Perhaps the earliest date that can be put to the Pilgrim's Way (and its fellow, the Icknield Way) is the Early Iron Age, but one would not have been able then to walk along them for miles without meeting anything but hares, conies or adders. Up to quite recent times the Drove Road (the Harroway which once linked the Channel with the Atlantic) was a populous thoroughfare, one kind of vagrant being succeeded by another, the pack-horse by the Welsh pony, the pardoner, the Franciscan, the chapman and the pedlar by the gipsies and the broomsquires. It was only yesterday that the drovers herded their ponies along the Hoar and Pilgrim Ways, just as the rhythmic plash of the water-wheel was heard in the Tillingbourne Valley during this very century. Now the millstones are only to be seen as flag or stepping stones in suburban gardens. It is possible, too, to guess at something of that busy active regional life which has vanished as though upset by an earthquake, by the surviving place-names. Abinger Hammer, of course, reveals the valley to have once been part of the great iron-working region of the Sussex Weald or Forest of Anderida, the Hammer Ponds being used for driving the water-wheels of the forges. In the swampy ground and by the banks of the valley stream that flows into the Tillingbourne grow many alders, the " fisherman's curse," with their triune knobbly fruits, and these were the favoured wood of the charcoal burners whose trade survived up to the end of the last war. It is difficult to believe now that these hammer ponds once lifted the tilt-hammers and filled the lungs of the bellows with air. Thus both oak and alder were the queen posts to the structure of a local industry. Ashes, too, supported it, so often to be seen in the neighbourhood of farmsteads, and even more of a boon and a blessing to the countryman than the Waverley pen to the townsman. They supplied the farm workers with the wood for their flails, their axe-hafts, their cart-shafts and their plough-beams, the thatcher with his " bow " for carrying the yealms up to the roof, the sower with his dibble, the shepherd with his " wattled cotes," the hurdler with his sheep-cribs. Many of the coppices in the valley are heavily stocked with holly, one of them near Abinger Mill nine feet high, and this is a clue to the number of " holms " (Holmbury) in the region. When the pilgrims set out along the Way from the old church at Shere, past Gomshall, and then north along Cold Kitchen Lane and east again to Ranmore Common, where I used to hear the woodlark singing, they were lamp-posted all the way by yews. The kindliness of the chalk to the yew is commemorated in Ewhurst, Ewell, Ewood Farm. Even to-day there is still a use for the hazel besides cracking its nuts, for there is one basketmaker left in the valley and he uses hazel, not withy as elsewhere, the thinnest laths being stripped with the teeth.

So the men of the valley and the slopes lived by the trees as the trees lived by the rock. " Thou canst not touch a flower without troubling of a star "—this is true of the universe *as a whole*, but in human life the only way of getting the measure of this wholeness is by belonging to a region to the full activity of its resources. The man who gets his beef from the Argentine, his bread from Canada, his sardines from the Mediterranean, his flowers from the Scillies, and his eggs from God knows where, belongs to nothing, not even to himself. He is a fragmented being for whom Cosmopolis is heaven and Cosmopolis is nowhere because it is everywhere. But what joy it is to go to a place and find out that you are somewhere ! In Surrey you have to look behind the scenes to find out where, so to speak, you are, and the trees give you an indication both of beginnings in the primeval rock and ends in the uses man has made of them. And Surrey is a region of great and noble trees—the sweet chestnuts of Burgate are some of the grandest trees that, as Pepys might have said, ever I saw in my life. It is fitting that Surrey was the county of Evelyn, perhaps the greatest of our dendrophilists, and doubtless many of the trees in and about the valley come of his planting from Wotton. Not only the trees, but the very look of the land with its intricate system of heights and bowl-like hollows, its tilted woodlands, little fields and abrupt changes of contour, its fussiness of outline, its deep-sunken winding lanes, very Devonian, its razor crests engraved with Scots pine, its oak and ash and chestnut and alder but no walnut, are all clues in the detective story. If one gets the hawk's view of Surrey and its neighbours from a point of vantage, say Newlands Corner, and can turn a blind eye to the bungalows, the petrol pumps, the villas, the reduplicated roads and all the other symptoms of otherness, then one can truly appreciate the difference between one stone and another, looking south to the long calm line of the South Downs behind the furry prickly sombre hump of Blackdown. One gathers the character of the Lower Greensand (Hythe Beds) in an eye-shot, its dendroculture, its hollows, marshes and commons, its secretive valleys, its sphinxlike headlands, and beyond its hummocky broken lines (very like what the Mendip people call " gruffy-ground " or disturbed land from old lead-mine workings) to the sea of Anderida and the cloud-contours of the chalk downs.

The rapid alternation of ridge and trough is accounted for by the variety of clays, sand and sandstone in the Lower Greensand. Rich meadow lands lie within the same small compass as Macbeth-like heaths with their broom, ling " hurts " (hurtleberry) and " goss." Indeed, it was in this region that Linnaeus went down on his knees before the gorse in flower. The sweet chestnut is here because it cannot endure lime; the old man's beard is on the chalk rotundities because it can hardly live without it. If you are looking for cowslips, the oaks will be a signpost to them, but for primroses you must step from one bed of stone to another. Nothing could be more unlike the pure chalk than this adulterate greensand.

It engenders no fewer than five kinds of building stone—liassic sandstone, ironstone, Merstham stone, Reigate stone, Horsham stone. Sarsen occurs at St. Martha's, but is a product as on the Marlborough Downs and elsewhere of the chalk. This bounty of the Greensand makes or made for a fine variety in the regional architecture. The ironstone, for instance, was much in use for "garreting" or "garnet-jointing," being driven into both the brick and the stone walls like tenpenny nails and, like the flush-work flint of East Anglia, producing a lively though less geometrical decoration. It may well have served, too, for holding the wall fast, since no rural industry has ever been ornamental alone. That was the achievement of the Industrial Revolution—to separate use from beauty, so that the one expressed itself in utilitarian ugliness and squalor, the other in frippery. How tenacious was the tradition of garreting may be gathered from the fifteen to twenty feet stone wall from which gushes the invisible stream near Gomshall, the sole relic of a thirteenth century priory. The unsightly house which now stands on its site was roofed with Norfolk reed-thatch costing £500—a notable example of what happens when nature's law and man's former law of using the materials proper to the region are violated. This house looks as I did when by mistake I went off with the wrong hat. The waste straw was thrown out as litter on the banks of a large goldfish pond, and is now a waving forest of reeds. Nature usually gets her own back in the end. Horsham stone, with its beautiful ripple markings, was much in favour for roofing churches, and to the eye of the faithful regionalist stands somewhere between the roof-slates of Cotswold colite and Purbeck limestone, an extremely heavy roofing stone. At Abinger Common there is a Lutyens house, of roughcast and tiling, by no means one of his best, but by it stands a wood shed of black weatherboarding and Horsham slats, or "healings" as they are locally known. This is a masterpiece in little, simply because it is a sympathetic modernization of the native style. The clay deposits on the Greensand allowed for brick-making, which in all districts that used to respect

their own integrity was used with russet roof-tiling.
With so rich a choice of building materials at his feet,
one can but imagine now the wealth of variation open to
and accepted by the local mason, but it was a variation
within the strictly defined limits of the region.   The
importing of Norfolk reed-thatch he would have considered an irresponsible lunacy.   Here and there the
regional discipline and the regional variety may be enjoyed,
at the domestic little Abinger Church, for instance, with
its oak-shingled pepper-pot spire, its weatherboarded
" tower," sandstone walls and Horsham slatted roof.
Or at the substantial yeoman's farmsteads of the valley.
I stayed in one of these, late Elizabethan it is, a quarter
of a mile away from Crossways Farm, of the same date,
the same brick and the same tenancy.   I did not know
that these were yeoman's farms by consulting parish
registers or local histories, but simply by their appearance,
the acreage of the land attached to them (often sixty
acres or half the " hide," which was the unit measurement
of a yeoman's holding), and the generous grouping of
barns and bartons.   The walls of these barns were
frequently garreted, and the timbers of the aisles bear the
mason's marks.

Diversity was indeed the seal of recognition for the
whole small region before modern uniformity swallowed
it up, and made it part of what Max Beerbolm once called
in my hearing " England's smooth and asphalt ground."
A diversity of soils, varying from the sandy waste to a
fecundity that is a gold-mine to the market gardener;
a diversity of landscape and contours; a diversity of
vegetation, a whole gamut from the bog-myrtle of the
swampy patches to the harebell, the butcher's broom,
the xerophytic sedums and the " hurts " of the arid uplands
which the gipsies used to sell at sixpence a basket full;
a diversity of trees—holly, alder, oak, sweet chestnut,
Scots pine, ash, elm, lime, of all Cobbett's favourites at
Farnham, of almost every tree Englishly extant except
the walnut; a diversity of buildings based on the
prodigality of the wherewithal to build them—what a little
dream Shere must have been once, half-timbering combined

with colour-washed brick, stone, tile-hanging and even flint, a captivating medley, the houses low, snug, homely, modest, and yet every one a striking and dependable individual. How enchanting is this combination of humility with individuality, of variety with obedience to the decree of the *place*—thus far but no further. I can't help thinking that the Irvingite church near the Silent Pool is not such a grotesque failure as it ought to be, totally out of keeping with the domestic little churches of the region as it is in its sham perpendicular Gothic, crocketed pinnacles and all, simply because it has caught the spirit of this prodigal variety which is Surrey as it once was. And lastly, a diversity of local crafts and industries. Nobody could possibly infer from anything they saw in the Valley of Tillingbourne or its tributary, or further afield, that this had once been a sheep country. They might guess it from the pastures of flaring ragwort, because ragwort often follows the abandonment of the sward by these living lawn-mowers. Curiously enough, the tradition was wheat and sheep, not barley and sheep as in the Chilterns and on the Berkshire Downs, and indeed on most of the light lands. At any rate, it was a strong tradition, for Aubrey speaks of the passage at Shere as " built on wool," and Banstead mutton was a name to conjure with. The many Tanners of the region (Tanhouse Farm, etc.), show that the saddlers did not have to go to some outlandish place for their leather, but that it came from the bark of their own oaks. Only one wheelwright survives in a region that might be called a *locus classicus* of this most English of crafts, since it was at Farnham a dozen miles away that George Sturt wrote his " The Wheelwright's Shop." Woodmanship in this richly wooded country has deteriorated to mere faggotting. The past laid a light finger on me when, on a visit, I caught a glimpse of the daughter of the woodman of Dearsleap on the Wotton estate, a very Tess with black hair and finely chiselled features. Even that was something; it reinforced my pet theory that in traditional wooding countries the craftsmen are, or were, descended in the long run from the Mediterraneans of the Neolithic era who escaped into the woods during the usurpations of the Iron Age. The dark-haired Neoliths were a race of superb craftsmen, and nearly all the woodsmen I know are Mediterranean types. A new kind of usurpation has banished not only the woodsmen but their crafts, the usurpation of money, machines and uniformity.

One of the things I did while I was in this valley was to visit " The Silent Pool." I had not seen it for nearly thirty years, and one of the very first things I ever wrote about our countryside had for its subject this secret place on the edge of the Albury Downs. Thus, a sentimental curiosity was strong enough to overcome a dislike for beauty spots which realizes what a price we have had to pay for regarding the country not as a home but a holiday, not as the scene of the Englishman's natural labours but as an escape from the unnatural and mechanical drudgery of a hypertrophied urban life. For that reason I have always done my best to avoid beauty spots where you go to inspect beauty in a herd, and gape at a pompous curator who expounds the points as though he were selling an incunabulum at Sotheby's. I do not enjoy admiring what I am told to admire. Still less do I like having England displayed before me as a museum piece, an entertainment, a recreation from the assembly line. What I like is the working England, the England whose beauty was a by-product of her utility for her own folk, the real England which happens to be the old England not because of " progress " but economic brigandage. This true England can never be " obsolete " because she was a contribution to eternal values, and compared with them industrialized bureaucratic England is only the scum that rides on the stream of time. It is pain, not pleasure, that I get out of beauty spots.

It was therefore with mixed feelings that I approached the Silent Pool, and the disagreeable ones were hardly allayed by my finding my foot upon a kind of cinder track running right round the upper and lower ponds. Still, there was nobody there, and to my enormous relief no official to babble bosh about King John and the beautiful maiden. There was no *tourisme* about to make one want to hide in the undergrowth. For the personally conducted tour was beautifully epitomized by William Blake :—

"He that bends to himself a joy
Doth the wingèd life destroy ;
But he that catches the joy as it flies
Lives in eternity's sunrise."

All of a sudden I became very happy, because there awoke in me what has long been obscured by the bitter need to walk along the dreary cinder-track of controversy, to be for ever fighting the enemies of English country—the pure enjoyment of the naturalist, without a thought, without a care in the world but to understand and appreciate what the old writers called "the works of creation." I felt an instant warm but reverent fellowship with all those serene figures (now, fortunately for them, in their graves) who have loved the peculiarly English stamp of Nature—Gilbert White, Linnæus, John Ray, Edmund Selous, Hudson, Jefferies, Charles Waterton, John Clare, Jesse Miller, Izaak Walton, Herrick. Chaucer, but, above all, Shakespeare, the more English for his universality, yes, and those wonderful old saints, Columba, Aidan, Cuthbert, and their kind, who settled on wild and rocky islets and by some miracle of devotion managed to scrape a living out of the stony soil. All naturalists in their way, even if some of them did believe that geese grew out of barnacles. The Silent Pool is surrounded by a dense vegetation and by trees, many of them that reach above a hundred feet. There is a Turkey oak there that need not have felt an inferiority complex had it been surrounded by giant tropical moras. Ashes, beeches, yews, girdling the still water, towered above it and burst, the deciduous ones, into flames of foliage that seemed nearer the sun than the soft mud that gave their roots such power. But a sight even more remarkable than their reflections in the green translucent water and the wood-nuts dangled right over it, was the old man's beard that shot up fifty feet out of the water in a solid wall of dense greenery. Actually, the water of this ancient Hammer Pond stands on the blue lias, so that the Pool occurs at the junction of the lias, the greensand and the chalk. There is always something peculiarly distinctive in land-surface about the meeting place between two or more strata, and here it was expressed by this cliff of tangled green descending sheer to the edge of a water as pellucid as that of a coral reef. The branches tossing above this cliff, the dark green pond-weeds and bright green cushions of potamogeton under the water, the stillness, the complete surround of enormous trees, the heavy shade, the clarity of the water, how could this be a scene in a suburbanized home county, when it was the glimpse of an Amazonian backwater and you expected to see turtles nosing up from the surface, and Bates appearing out of the greenery with his spectacles on his nose and his band of Indians behind him? But for turtles there were great otiose trout, as comfortable and leisurely as monastic carp, occasionally rising to send fat wide symmetrical ripples from glassy surface to green-walled banks. Apollinaris Sidonius, writing in the fourth century A.D., might have been describing the Silent Pool: " The shallows along the banks look green ; overarching boughs lend the water their own hues and the water transmits it to the pebbles at the bottom."

So there really was once an ancient Surrey. What an adventure she must have been for the dark Iberians drifting along the Ridge Way above the valley, for the red-headed Goidels forging the iron for their stirrups in her forests, for the Saxons clearing them for their first settlements along her streams, for the medieval masons mining the wealth of her soils for their godly buildings, for Chaucer's Pilgrims, for Evelyn compiling his *Kalendarium hortense* at Albury, for the children who picked the " hurts " and the cottagers who made wine out of them, for the glass-makers and the leather-workers, the tanner and the wheelwright, for all the children of her woods and wastes and meadows, who were not yet her prodigal sons who left her for the city and returned not to repent but to despoil her.

CINDERELLA

By LORD MOTTISTONE
(General Jack Seely)

Thirty-eight years ago in a remote oasis in Upper Egypt an Arab chieftain said this to me : " Your people treat the dog as your friend, and the horse as your slave. With us Arabs it is the other way. Ours is the better plan."

My English readers may guess that I replied to his first statement : " Could not one make both the horse and the dog one's friend ? "

He replied : " No, every man should have one horse that he cares for beyond anything else. If he makes friends with a dog the horse will know, and he may lose the friendship of the horse."

I have arrived at this conclusion. If a man is to be completely happy he must have : of horses, one real friend and only one ; of women, one real friend, his wife, and only one ; of all the rest one may seek safety and happiness in numbers, but not for those two.

I HAD just returned from the South African War, where all of us young men thought we had become preternaturally observant. Each one of us who had commanded advance guards of mounted men during that long struggle, in which we learned to admire our enemies more and more, thought himself the embodiment of Sherlock Holmes. No doubt it was true that anyone who had the lives of a squadron of men and horses committed to his care, leading them forward in that mysterious country—the High Veldt of South Africa—did, indeed, have his wits sharpened to an extraordinary degree. It was a game of everlasting hide and seek. Ultimately the overwhelming superiority was with the English, but locally it was often on the side of the Dutch. All the time an immense advantage lay with the Dutchman, not so much in his knowledge of the country, as in his knowledge of the horse—how to manage him, how to care for him, how to keep him quiet at the tense moment before fire opens, how to prevent him from trembling, or, worst of all, from stampeding when fire opens unexpectedly. All these things the Dutchman knew far better than we did. It was from the Dutch, and especially from the greatest of them all, in the end England's good and faithful friend, General Botha, that I learnt the supreme value of understanding and caring for the horse, and of treating him not as a slave but as a brother.

In the foreword I have described the moment in my life when an Arab of the desert first opened my eyes to the possibilities of companionship with the horse. That was ten years before the time of which I speak; it was in South Africa that I learnt that the Arab's dictum was true.

And so it came about that Cinderella, Warrior's mother, came into my keeping in the strange way that she did, through the power of observation that I had picked up in South Africa.

In August, 1902, the yeomanry regiment to which I belonged, the Hampshire Carabineers, was in camp on Salisbury Plain. I had been promoted to command a squadron on my return from the War, and was sitting on the top of Silk Hill, having been ordered to plan a field-day for the following morning.

I was surveying the well-known landscape with my 24-diameter telescope, the present of a famous deer-stalker, which was of constant value to me in South Africa and in the late War, and has been ever since. On my left, as I sat there with my Arab pony, Maharajah, a little cloud of dust caught my eye. The telescope showed me that it was a man galloping at great speed. As he drew nearer I saw that it was an officer in khaki uniform mounted on a black horse with long mane and tail. They passed within three hundred yards of me at the foot of the hill, and I recognized the smooth effortless gallop of a perfectly trained thoroughbred on terms with his rider.

My father had told me that he would give me a charger. My mind was made up. This must be my charger! Clearly the man would not be galloping like this, all alone,

CINDERELLA AND HER FOAL WARRIOR

(*Copied from the original by A. J. Munnings, R.A.*)

unless he knew that his horse was perfectly sound in wind and limb, nor would he be sitting so easily in the saddle unless he were sure that his horse would not attempt to run away with him.

So I jumped on to Maharajah's back and galloped sideways down the hill to try to catch him up. Eventually the black thoroughbred, as I made it out to be, slowed down, and I ranged up alongside the rider.

This was our conversation :

" Would you sell that horse of yours ? "

" It isn't a horse, it's a mare."

" I'm sorry, but will you sell that mare ? "

" Well, I might."

" How much ? "

" Seventy pounds."

" I would have given you ninety or a hundred ; but will you ride over to my camp at once ? "

" You're an odd young man."

" I'm sorry, but you have a lovely mare."

" Yes, she is a lovely mare. The kindest thing I have ever known."

So we rode back over the hill where I had been sitting, and down to the camp. On the way he told me something of Cinderella's story—how she was a clean-bred mare from County Leitrim, how he had bought her for £60, six months before, from the famous Mr. Field, of Chichester, how she was almost human, and would follow him about like a dog. As he talked Cinderella would cock one ear back, and listen to his voice.

I remembered what my Arab friend had told me, and by that time would have sold all my few possessions in order that Cinderella might be mine.

And so we rode down to our camp on that glorious August morning, and jumped off at my tent.

My faithful orderly of South African days, Smith, came forward and took both horses, and I invited my guest inside to have a whisky and soda. While we sat there waiting for it to come, I asked him again :

" Did you say seventy pounds ? "

" Yes, I said seventy."

I wrote him a cheque for eighty and handed it to him.

" But why the extra tenner ? "

" Because I am going to keep your lovely Cinderella here, and you can ride back on some other horse which I will lend you."

He laughed at my enthusiasm, and accepted the cheque, protesting as he rode away on the pony I lent him that he would send me back ten pounds any time that I wished.

So Warrior's mother came to belong to me, and, in a curious way, so far as there can be true affinity between man and horse, I to her.

Her story is romantic, and ends on a sad note, but on this first day, without doubt, it can be said that it was a happy chance that brought us two together.

How well I remember on that Summer's morning, in camp on Salisbury Plain, leading my new charger to the horse-lines, where about four hundred other horses were tethered by a headstall and a hind leg to long ropes pegged down to the ground. I saw Cinderella looking at me all the time and wondering what was in store for her. By great good fortune, tethered on the very end of the rope was my white Arab pony, Maharajah, that I had ridden constantly for a year and a half in the South African War. He had left the Isle of Wight with me at the end of 1899, and after much trekking over the South African veldt, and many battles, which we now regard as small, but some of which we then regarded as very important, he had returned with me once more in 1901.

I had followed the advice of the Arab chieftain, whose words I quoted at the beginning of this story, in every particular with Maharajah, who was indeed my friend, and would never leave me even when loose and free from all control. He was just such a companion as a dog can be, but more intimate, and a closer friend.

Maharajah whinnied when I came up to the horse-lines, then looked round, and saw the beautiful, coal-black mare with the glossy coat and clear, wide-open eye of the Arab. I wondered what would happen, and expected the worst, for Maharajah, like all horses who become friendly with men or women, was jealous of any rival.

My faithful groom and orderly, who had been with me
and Maharajah during our long service together in South
Africa, accompanied me on this adventure. We both
made endearing remarks to Maharajah, but I could plainly
see a wicked look in his eye. I handed my sleek new
thoroughbred to Smith, and told him to tie her up to the
head-rope four feet from Maharajah while I went forward,
patted his neck, and tried to explain to him that he had a
nice new friend coming to see him. He trembled a little,
and refused a lump of sugar which I had brought to offer
him in order to effect a friendship. Then I stepped
back while the tying up of the headstall and the hind leg
was accomplished.

Cinderella never turned her head to look at Maharajah,
nor did Maharajah, four feet away, pay the least attention
to her. Then I made a mistake. I went forward and
fondled Cinderella's head and ears, and with a pat for
Maharajah turned about and walked away. I had not
gone ten yards when there was a scream; Maharajah
had broken his headstall, and had caught Cinderella's
wither firmly in his teeth ! I dashed back to them, and
they were soon separated. It was the first and last occasion
on which they quarrelled, for, from that moment, they
became inseparable friends. When I rode one the other
followed; I have never known two horses so deeply
attached to one another.

Human beings will not realize that the affections of
horses are much more closely akin to their own than is
the case with any other creature. The Arab knows this,
and treats them as human beings. Europeans think
that the Arabs are, as they phrase it, " mad about horses."
It is we and not the Arabs who are mad in our dealings
with these the most mysterious, and most lovable, of all
God's creatures.

From that moment Cinderella was my constant companion and friend until the outbreak of the recent War.
Maharajah showed discernment in his affection for her,
for she was the gentlest, kindliest creature that I have
ever known, especially beloved by children. She would
let my children climb up over her head, and slide down

G

her tail and, still more remarkable, swarm up her tail and slide down over her head. But she had a fine turn of speed, and though only standing fifteen hands, could, I think, have won a good race. At any rate, I was often begged to allow her to try.

She came back with Maharajah and me to the Isle of Wight, where she was to spend most of her life. Whether it was the change from being one of a " string," that hateful phrase, to being one of two in constant touch with her friend called the " owner," I do not know, but the fact is that this lovely, docile, black thoroughbred became so devoted to me that she could not bear to leave me. My elder children will testify that whenever she saw me she would jump out of any enclosure, even over an iron railing, in order to join me.

As Maharajah became too old to attend manœuvres and staff rides, Cinderella took his place. When I became a Minister, Cinderella came to London with me, and I used to ride her every morning to the Colonial Office, after a gallop round the Park if I got up early enough—a rare occasion. But she did not like London, and was never really happy there. Of course, when the Parliamentary recess came we enjoyed ourselves thoroughly in the Isle of Wight, riding over the downs or galloping over the sands at Brooke and Compton, and sometimes taking a day with the Isle of Wight Hunt. But although she could gallop fast, and jump well, I knew she did not care for these days with hounds. What she really loved was to be alone with me in the sun or the rain, and, above all, in the great south-west winds. It was in days of storm that she sprang to life ; she loved the strong west wind. I see her now with distended nostrils, black mane and tail streaming, galloping through the gale and rejoicing in her strength.

Meantime her comrade, Maharajah, the white Arab, whom she had first met on Salisbury Plain, and who had been her constant companion in the Isle of Wight, while they were turned out together on the cliff as often as might be, slipped up one frosty morning, crossed his legs and broke his neck. The school-children were all looking on, and Maharajah loved to give them a show, jumping over imaginary obstacles, galloping on his forelegs while whisking his hindquarters round and round as only Arabs can do. It was in doing this particular trick that he slipped on the icy ground and met his end. But Cinderella was looking on too ; she was broken-hearted, and wandered listless and gloomy for day after day, refusing to take any food offered to her.

Then " Young Jim," my constant adviser in anything connected with horses, had a great idea. Obviously so wonderful a creature should have a child, and so in 1906 she was mated with a horse named Likely Bird. She went to Yafford for the event, and, in due course, a handsome son was born within sound of the sea. " Young Jim," and all concerned, thought this was the best foal ever seen, but, unfortunately, the brilliant young thing caught a chill of some kind, and died suddenly, to the disappointment of the Jolliffe family, and to the real grief of his mother, Cinderella.

I saw her often at this time, and, though it is difficult for human and equine creatures to communicate with each other, I like to think that she was somewhat consoled by our interviews in those grass fields stretching down to the sea at Yafford. But more real consolation was provided by another mate. This time it was Straybit who was destined to be the father of her foal.

Straybit was an exceptionally bright chestnut. I never saw a better-looking horse. By breeding he had every advantage. His father was Burnaby, his mother was Myrthe.

Before me as I write I see among his ancestors the names of such famous horses as Voltigeur, winner of the Derby and the St. Leger in 1850, Lowlander, The Baron, Stockwell and Pocahontas. Straybit was indeed bred for speed, but it is interesting to note that more than one of those who keep careful account of our great English thoroughbreds have told me that his ancestors include an exceptional number of horses and mares well-known for their gentleness and docility.

For although so handsome and so swift, Straybit was

of an exceptionally kindly nature. "Young Jim," who looked after him, as well as Cinderella and their child, Warrior, tells me that not only did he ride him in several races, but he was so quiet that he even went to the length of putting him in harness just for fun.

This particular adventure was not a success. Straybit went along quietly enough with this strange thing—a dog-cart—behind him until something displeased him, probably the crupper. In spite of the efforts of "Young Jim" and two other people, Straybit just set to work to get rid of that dog-cart as fast as he could, a feat which he accomplished with no damage to himself, and very little to the men who tried to restrain him, though they found themselves in a ditch; but the dog-cart was never the same again! However, this was the only occasion when Straybit lost his temper.

One very interesting episode in his life occurred in the Spring of 1909. He won the Lightweight Race at the Isle of Wight Point-to-Point, the same race that his little son Warrior was destined to win, after four years of the Great War, in 1922. On both occasions "Young Jim" was the successful rider.

In the December after he won the Isle of Wight Point-to-Point he went to the blood-stock sales at Newmarket, where he was bought at a good price by the Austrian Government. I have heard that he was a very successful sire, and sometimes I wonder whether Warrior may not, in the course of the War, have met, at fairly close quarters, his half-brothers and half-sisters, or even his father himself. We do know that the Austrians provided a great number of horses to the German army, so such a happening is not impossible.

However, the main importance of Straybit to Cinderella and to me lay in the fact that he was the father of Warrior.

How well I remember receiving the telegram at the Colonial Office, where I was then installed as Under-Secretary of State, announcing :

"Fine child for Cinderella born at Yafford this morning. Both doing well.—JIM."

My private secretary brought me the telegram, and

looked at me narrowly. He was an austere man, R. V. Vernon, a most distinguished civil servant, and until lately our financial advisor in Iraq. I shouted with joy, and then turned on him and told him that Cinderella was a mare. But as he retired demurely I knew that he did not believe a word of what I said !

Yafford is one of the most delightful places that one could choose to possess as a birthplace. The thatched farm buildings where Warrior was born look just the same to-day as they did twenty-six years ago, even to the chickens scratching in the yard outside.

In due course Warrior was weaned, and with his mother roamed the fields at Brooke and Mottistone, till she once more resumed her duties as my charger.

Then, in August, 1914, Warrior went to the War with me and Cinderella was left behind in the Isle of Wight, turned out in the big grass fields adjoining Brooke and Mottistone, wherever the pasture was best. Again, as when Maharajah was killed, she became listless and moody, missing not only me, her friend for twelve long years, but her son with whom she had been, with some intervals, for more than four years past. My children did their best to look after her, and to cheer her up, but for the first month or two she seemed inconsolable. However, the World War had a curious consequence for Cinderella and provided her with some consolations.

Warrior and I having gone to the Front, Cinderella spent most of her time alone, turned out in the great field called " Sidling Paul." Now my father had a good breed of very powerful cart-horses, in which he took a great interest. One thing that made it necessary for these cart-horses to be very strong was the existence of the Brooke lifeboat. It took ten horses to haul the heavy boat on its carriage along the loose sand to the point of launching, but even with ten horses, unless each one was powerful, and they all pulled as a team, the boat was liable to get stuck. Such a team was always forthcoming in my father's time, and, indeed, until a year ago, when we replaced the horses with a tractor.

I suppose things were a little disorganized in September,

1914, but, whatever the explanation, a very fine entire cart foal was turned out on " Sidling Paul " too. No doubt it was assumed that Cinderella was much too old to have another child, but it happened otherwise.

When I came home on short leave in the Summer of 1915 almost the first question I asked was, " How is Cinderella ? " The children replied with glee :

" Cinderella has had a baby and we have christened it Isaac."

" Why Isaac ? "

" Well, we thought she must be almost as old as Sarah was in the Bible ! Come and see him."

So we walked up to the paddock between the house and the church. There was Cinderella, who, seeing me, neighed and cantered up. Sure enough, she was followed by a young foal. It had a sweet little head, as all foals have, but the most comically hairy legs and heels ! I fondled Cinderella as she rubbed her head against my shoulder, while the foal surveyed us both with interest. I could not help laughing when I looked at its hairy legs, and I am sure Cinderella was hurt, for she turned away from me, and licked her child's shoulder. However, I called him endearing names, and made him suck a lump of sugar, so that Cinderella resumed her equanimity, and walked back with me towards the house.

I went through the kissing-gate into the garden, and was walking up the path towards the house when I heard a rat-tat behind me. I looked round and saw that the foal had jumped the iron railing, and was trotting up to us, to the consternation of his mother, who realized that she could not follow.

However, we soon lifted the kissing-gate off its hinges, and restored them to each other.

I had to return to France two days later, and so saw no more of Isaac ; and, to my infinite regret, I saw but little more of Cinderella either, for the end of her story is sad. She was devoted to her quaint child ; the very fact that everyone laughed about the episode made her more than ever determined to be kind to the little animal. My children and the farm bailiff concur in saying that they never saw a mare so devoted to her foal. But shortly after Isaac had been weaned, his passion for jumping was his undoing. In trying to jump a very high fence out of the paddock he caught his forefeet, fell, and broke his neck.

So Cinderella was more than ever lonely, except for the constant attention of the children.

I did not see her again until 1916. It was late on a Summer's evening, and pale shafts of sunlight shone through the trees. As soon as I reached home I asked the children how was Cinderella? They said she seemed rather feeble, and was in the field by the church path. So I walked up there, and saw her, standing very erect with arched neck—I suppose she had heard my step on the gravel path. I gave her a shout, our agreed shout, and she looked my way. I gave another shout, and then she knew. But this time she could not canter; she trotted up to me and gave me a greeting so affectionate, so moving in its intensity, that I can never forget it. I talked to her for a long time, stroking her nose, before turning home.

Early the next morning my son Patrick, then a little boy of eleven, came knocking at my door and shouting:

"Daddy, there is something wrong with Cinderella."

I jumped up, and ran out to the field where I had left her the evening before. There, lying on the church path, was Cinderella. I knew at once that she was dead. I suppose that for all that long year she had waited to see me.

It was a Sunday morning, and we had to pass her body on our way to church. Soon after midday I received the inevitable telegram, which all who served in the War will still remember so well, ordering me to return at once. I left immediately and got back to France the same night. On the Monday Cinderella was buried.

Reprinted from " My Horse Warrior " by permission of Lord Mottistone and Messrs. Hodder and Stoughton.

THE
SCANDALOUS CUCKOO

By FRANCES PITT

THERE is no more scandalous bird than the cuckoo. By no standard of conduct, whether human or animal, can its habits of life be condoned.

Whereas the majority of birds pair respectably, often marrying for life, the cuckoo knows naught of marital ties ; and as for its offspring, we are all aware how it foists its eggs upon other birds and leaves them to bring up the young ones.

But let us start with the migrant cuckoo flying back from overseas to that corner of the English countryside which it regards as home. This return usually takes place during the latter part of April and early May. There are records of March cuckoos, and still earlier ones have been reported, but the cuckoo's well-known call is easy to imitate, and many an early-arrived cuckoo has on investigation resolved itself into a small boy hidden behind a bush.

As a rule the cuckoo delays its return until the primroses

are thick on the hedgebanks, until the buds on the trees
are breaking into greenery and Spring is really here.
Then comes the familiar cry "cuc-koo! cuc-koo!"—
that call which seems the very spirit of the English Spring,
which seems likewise to tell of the rising tide of life and
all the joy of the season.

Soon we catch a glimpse of a hawk-like form flitting
from tree to tree, so hawk-like that in days of old the
country folk firmly believed that the Winter disappearance
of the cuckoo was due to it turning into a hawk. This
belief persisted until comparatively recently. I well
remember as a small child being told in all seriousness
by an old countryman how the one bird could be transformed into the other; yet, seen near at hand, the cuckoo's
grey-blue form has more likeness to that of a pigeon.

For the first few days of its homecoming we hear only
the characteristic call from which the cuckoo takes its
name. This may be due, as is the case with many species
of migrant birds, to the males arriving before the females.
At any rate, we usually have to wait a little for another
sound to come down the Spring-time breeze—a lovely
bubbling call, a noise as of running, gurgling water;
in short, the cry of the hen cuckoo.

Whether the female cuckoo can also utter the "cuc-koo"
call I do not know. Many observers say "No," but it is
not easy to prove the negative.

Here the lady comes, flying in a lazy, idle, languid
manner, and after her fly two more cuckoos, for it must
be confessed that she is a dame of several loves and has
generally more than one swain in attendance. The
female cuckoo does not mate, but is polyandrous, or
perhaps it is more correct to say that she is promiscuous,
flirting lightly with any male who comes along. After
all, pairing is just a matter of partnership to ensure the
welfare of the future family, and where family responsibilities are cast aside, what need is there to take a mate?

The newly-arrived female cuckoo has, however, matters
which must be attended to, namely, the disposal of her
eggs, and here it seems that heredity plus individual habit
has some influence.

There are hedge-sparrow cuckoos, meadow pipit cuckoos, those that patronize reed warblers, etc. ; that is there are birds which confine themselves to particular species and specialize in duping them. Cuckoo's eggs vary tremendously in colour and markings, and some naturalists have gone so far as to aver that the cuckoo adapts the colour of her egg to that of the fosterer ; but we have no scientific evidence that any bird can control the colour and markings of her egg. The most frequent type of cuckoo egg in this country is a mottled one resembling that of the pied wagtail. I have seen eggs of this description inserted in the nests of the robin, wagtail, and hedge sparrow, with equal success.

It is not the least amazing thing about this amazing bird that its victims rarely, if ever, refuse the egg which is foisted upon them. The cuckoo keeps watch upon the small birds of her district, especially the kind she prefers, notes where different pairs are preparing nests, and when a nest is ready—that is, has received three or four eggs of the clutch it is to contain—glides down, removes an egg, and deposits one of her own.

There is great argument among naturalists as to whether the cuckoo lays her egg direct into the nest or sometimes deposits it at a distance, picks it up, and carries it in her beak to the nest. Certainly cuckoo eggs have been discovered in situations where it seems impossible for the cuckoo to have found ingress, but it is a fact that she can do extraordinarily acrobatic feats. In some cases where the bird has been seen with an egg in her beak, it has almost certainly been one filched from her victim.

In the course of the season a hen cuckoo lays a considerable number of eggs, up to twenty-one from one bird having been recorded, but that was in especially favourable circumstances—in the course of Mr. Edgar Chance's well-known experiments. Probably ten to a dozen eggs is nearer the average for the rank and file of the cuckoo clan ; that is upwards of a dozen eggs are foisted on small birds, which meekly accept the burden.

The foster parents proceed with incubation in the normal manner until, some twelve to thirteen days later, hatching time arrives—that of their own and the alien egg. Out tumbles that repulsive little monster, the baby cuckoo; out likewise tumble their own hapless young ones.

Allowing for sentiment, allowing for prejudice aroused by its behaviour, it remains a fact that the juvenile cuckoo is as ugly a little horror as can be found among young birds, a shapeless, top-heavy, head-heavy wretch, yet endowed with a strange activity and irritability. When anything touches it it begins to fidget. The adjoining nestlings drive it to great contortions; it wriggles and shoves, gets beneath one, and with skinny wings extended, head wobbling and its feeble legs spread, works its way backwards up the side of the nest, to spill its burden overboard. Thus, one after the other, it gets its foster brothers and sisters upon its back and ejects them from the home.

Strange indeed is the mind of a bird. While this gruesome tragedy proceeds the parents come unheeding to the nest, they feed their changeling child, they feed such of their right....al babies as are still with them, they brood the survivors, and never heed those that lie dying on the ground below or even on the verge of the nest. Once a nestling has departed from the cup of the nest it seems to have passed outside their comprehension and consciousness. In a few short hours all the little ones have gone, have perished of exposure, while the cuckoo snuggles beneath the protecting warmth of its foster-mother's breast.

Having now the undivided attention of the foster-parents, the young cuckoo flourishes amazingly, swells as rapidly as a balloon being blown up, gains feathers, and fills the nest almost to overflowing. The misguided, deluded birds lavish more and more attention upon it. They ply it with grubs and insects of all sorts, and still it grows. There comes a day when it flaps its wings, feels their strength and flies out into the world. Are its slaves released? By no means. It is now, as it leaves the nest, that the cuckoo finds its voice, an insistent, penetrating squeak, repeated at short intervals, which squeak brings its doting foster-parents flying in its wake. They follow it, and still they ply it with food, and—perhaps most scandalous of the many scandalous happenings in the life of this reprehensible bird—sometimes other birds come and help them.

That insistent squeak seems to have a magic quality. It touches some chord in the heart of the small bird which is irresistible. I have watched a robin stuffing a young cuckoo which had fled from a pied wagtail's nest and which had its foster-parents in attendance.

After several days of this sort of thing even the young cuckoo begins to find its own food. The slaves, their season's work thrown away on a parasite, are released at last and retire to moult and recuperate.

In the meantime, what of the old cuckoos? They, too, their season's business so easily disposed of, have been moulting and are now leaving for foreign shores. There is nothing to detain them. They have no ties, and they are among the earliest of the migrant birds to move off south.

The young cuckoo, yet in the dark barred and speckled plumage which is quite different from that of its elders, tarries awhile, idling about the countryside and gaining strength and experience. August passes into September, and then it, too, feels the urge to be up and off. Alone, without parents or foster-parents, it flies away, driven by those inherited forces of which we know so little, and leaving us with yet another marvel, the southward migration of these immature birds.

Rogue as it is, the cuckoo presents us with some of the strangest problems in Nature, not the least being the journey south of its lonely young one and the probability that it will return to the district where it was bred. How does it find its way back?

MANX SHEARWATERS

AFTER DARK

By Frances Pitt

Many are the creatures which hold revel when the sun
has set, from the household pussy who forgets her sedate
fireside demeanour and glides off down the garden path,
across the meadow and away into the woods, to such
birds as the owls and the nightjar, and such animals as
the fox and the badger.

The bats, which we are accustomed to think of as
creatures of the night, do not really belong to the dark
hours, for most of them fly at dusk and again at dawn,
resting in their dens during the middle of the night;
nevertheless, as they do not come out until sundown
and often fly on, in joyous chase of the evening insects,

until it is so dark one can barely see their shapes as they
dash by against the sky, they must have mention, for they
hold high revel indeed.

On late Summer evenings they are very active, and a
twilight stroll around the garden is sure to reveal many of
them.   When I was out one night there were sundry tiny
bats flitting to and fro about the creepers on the house,
darting close to me with eerie rustlings of skinny wings,
and anon appearing as momentary silhouettes against the
fast darkening sky, upon the purple ground of which the
winking stars grew thicker every moment.   Away to
the north-west the sky was lighter, a pallid lemon-green
becoming orange at its verge where the sun had dropped
from sight in golden glory.   Across this sunset sky passed
the shape of a large bat flying high and swiftly, which
must have been a noctule, or great bat, just as the tiny
bats about the house were certainly pipistrelles, or flittermice, to give them their country name.

I then betook myself to the bushes by the pond-side,
where again there was much business, the rustling of
wings as bats dived headlong, and the squeaking of
their tiny voices as they chased each other merrily over
the water.

There were two or three bats hawking for insects
around the trees, threading their way through the branches
with uncanny skill, and sometimes swooping quite near.
At last I got a view of one, and knew it for that strange
gnome of the twilight, the long-eared bat.

What a fantastic wee beast is this bat with those amazing
ears that seem developed out of all proportion. They
are nearly as long as itself !   Yet they are beautiful, being
exquisitely delicate and sensitive, and for ever on the
move.   The bat is always waving them to and fro, furling
and unfurling them, and seems to use them as feelers as
well as organs of hearing.   Many people believe that it is
its ears, used as marvellously sensitive tactile organs,
which enable this bat to thread its way in and out of the
branches and round about the trees in the manner which
it loves to do, and in illumination so poor that a human
being can hardly see at all.

But there are many other sounds to be heard after dark on an August evening besides the rustling of bat wings and shrill cries. There is that strange and persistent " churring " of the nightjar, or fern-owl, which goes on and on, now seeming to come from here, now from there, but ever difficult to locate.

I once spent a night out—a glorious warm Summer night—on a Welsh island, and from dusk to dawn two pairs of these birds kept up their weird noise. Save when one caught a glimpse of a bat-like shape against the sky, one never saw them, but the shadows were ever filled by the ventriloquial sound.

This night visit was to try to locate a colony of that bird of the dark, the Manx shearwater. This shearwater, like many of its cousins of the petrel family, does not believe in daylight visits to the nursery. By day it skims the waves on tireless wings, and only ventures shorewards under cloak of darkness, dashing excitedly through the gloom with cries like that of a bantam cock crowing.

My friend and I heard no crowing on the night in question, only the " churring " of the fern-owls above the dew-soaked bracken, but afterwards we visited an island where the Manx shearwater breeds in thousands, and the tiny storm petrel, or Mother Carey's chicken, comes likewise in large numbers—an amazing spot with a great population, but little sign is there by day of petrels or shearwaters. Gulls—greater, lesser, black-backed and herring—are there in great numbers ; razorbills, puffins and guillemots throng the cliffs ; but the only hint of underground life is the numerous well-used burrows, the ground in many places being honeycombed with holes. Here and there, it is true, you come across the poor remains, just dry bones and a few feathers, of what was once a shearwater, a victim of those arch pirates the great black-backed gulls.

Maybe it is the presence of these bloodthirsty scoundrels which makes midnight visits imperative, for once on the ground the shearwaters are awkward, clumsy, helpless birds. Be that as it may, the fact remains that no Manx

shearwater nor storm petrel ventures ashore while daylight
remains.

The shearwaters begin to collect in the early evening
off their island home, flock after flock coming in until
a great host of birds has assembled, and so they wait while
the sun sinks, the sunset fades from the sky, and the
shadows of night descend. Even then they are in no
hurry, and it is not until night has quite come that
they really begin business.

The first night that I went out it was a perfect evening,
still and dark, the sea gleaming grey and flecked here
and there with the distant winking of the lighthouses,
while on all sides resounded the voices of the shearwaters.
The crowing came from below, sitting birds crying to
their mates ; from above, the incoming birds screaming
that they were at hand ; and from the fern, wherein many
shearwaters were scuttling about like rabbits.

Now and again a bird would hurtle by so close that its
wings brushed one's face, and then a shearwater really
bumped into me. Storm petrels, neither so noisy nor so
noticeable, were also present in some numbers, and kept
flitting around, visible now and again as dark shapes
against the stars.

The clamour of the shearwaters was incessant, and
with it mingled the voices of restless gulls and the whistle
of an unsleeping oyster-catcher.

We approached an open space, a veritable shearwater
town, where the ground was honeycombed with burrows,
and walking without the aid of a torch was fraught with
difficulty. I tumbled from one hole into another, switched
on the light and saw scores of shearwaters sitting before
the burrows or running awkwardly about.

Yet, however busy this scene, the same spot was even
busier when I visited it at the hour of departure, when
the outgoing birds were in a desperate hurry to get off
and away to sea ere the sun rose and the dreadful gulls
caught them.

The shearwaters scuttled across the open ground,
making for a ridge of rock, up which they scrambled
surprisingly briskly for such seemingly awkward birds.

They are, in fact, very clumsy on land, and have great difficulty in taking wing from a level surface, hence the reason for their anxiety to get up the rocks. Once on the top and they could launch themselves with ease.

We were near the lighthouse, which at regular intervals flashed a rosy gleam upon the scene, revealing birds here and there, hurrying over the broken ground, hastening to the departure rock and scrambling even more hurriedly up it. There was a steady stream of shearwaters until a hint of coming dawn paled the north-eastern sky and a chill breath of air smote the cheek. Day was at hand and the last birds hurried off, desperate to be gone before light came.

As we made our way home a few belated shearwaters scuttled back down the burrows, and one or two hustled into the fern, seeming aware of their danger should sunrise and the gulls find them in the open.

It is probable that it is this danger of daytime visits to the nesting burrows that has forced the shearwater to nocturnal habits, but why many inland creatures love the night is not so certain.

The owls do so because their quarry, the mice, run about under cover of darkness, but the badger could get a living just as well by day and is strong enough and large enough to fear nothing, nevertheless, it is the most strictly nocturnal of creatures. I fancy the fact is that, despite its bulk and its well-armed jaws, the badger is so shy and inoffensive an animal that it likes to do its travelling and foraging when it will not be seen, hence it rarely leaves home until after sundown and makes a point of being back before sunrise.

Only once have I caught a badger going home in the dawn. It was a misty, late Summer morning, the dew was white upon the turf, the spiders' webs hung everywhere like magic lace, and wisps of fog hung in the hollows. The sun was rising like a fiery ball, driving beams through the mists and making a path of shimmering glory across the gossamer-laced herbage, when through the thistles and bracken by the hedge hurried a grey, bulky shape. I had but a fleeting glimpse of " Squire Brock " as he bolted for the woods.

H

THE LITTLE BROWN ELF

By FRANCES PITT

A SMALL cardboard box was thrust into my hands. It was pricked with holes, tied up with string (firmly knotted), and an anxious voice said, "Don't let it out!" But I was already working at the knots, which were complicated. They were untied at last, and I cautiously raised the lid of the box to reveal a wee creature, that tiny scrap of life and silky brown fur which is known to naturalists as a pipistrelle, to the country folk as a flittermouse or leathery bat, and to others merely as "a bat."

I gazed at the tiny thing, which, as it huddled in the corner of the box with wings folded away, looked small indeed, and marvelled that energy, high spirits, and joyous vitality could be generated in so wee a frame. At the moment the bat did not look joyous; indeed, it looked miserable. It raised a tiny face, a strange snub-nosed countenance which reminded one of an elfish bulldog, and its little jaws moved, showing incredibly miniature teeth.

It may have said something, for bats utter shrill sounds, perhaps many above the capacity of the human ear. For we know that even their ordinary cries, uttered as they fly through the dusk, are inaudible to most persons over forty years of age. To the boy and girl the twilight resounds with excited cries, cries of the chase and of mate calling to mate, but to the elder the night is silent, hence I suspect that the pipistrelle in the box was uttering remarks too high-pitched for the ears around it.

What a world of sound and vibration must be open to these sensitive beings. I moved a piece of paper across the table. To me the sound was slight. The bat quivered as if it had received a blow, and shrank back into its corner. Later I repeated the experiment, and again the little animal quivered visibly. It was obviously deeply affected by every noise.

I put it in a quiet place and considered what was to be done with it. I wanted to keep it for a few hours at any rate, and take a photograph before letting it go. It had been found sheltering behind a blind, hung up by its heels, half asleep in a dark corner. No doubt it had been making its home there. All bats, even the wee pipistrelles, have their dens in which they spend the day and much of the night. The latter remark may make persons who are accustomed to think of bats as creatures of the dark exclaim, but the fact is that bats are mostly animals of the twilight. They leave their retreats as the light begins to fade, enjoy a hectic hour, go home, rest awhile, and come forth again in the dawn. They do not usually fly the night through.

Perhaps they find this too tiring, perhaps the duration of their flight is governed by that of the insects they hunt, for the bats are mighty hunters of the gauzy throng that mount the evening air—from that queer gnome of the twilight, the long-eared bat which pursues moths around the bushes, to the powerful noctule, or great bat, which courses on strong wings high overhead after the insects that go aloft.

We have some dozen species of bats recognized as British, of which the pipistrelle, the whiskered bat, the noctule, and the long-eared bat are fairly frequent. The peculiar horse-shoe bats, the greater and lesser, are also not uncommon in cave districts. They owe their name to the leaf-like horse-shoe shaped appendages they wear upon the nose. Yet for queerness I do not think they eclipse the long-eared bat, with its immense ears, like great sensitive feelers, that during the bat's active hours are for ever being furled and unfurled.

I give the long-eared bat pride of place among our bats for strangeness and uncanniness, but for dainty appeal I prefer the little brown elf of the twilight, even when a protesting prisoner in a cardboard box.

Prisoners must be looked after, so I sought for flies, remembering a previous pipistrelle I kept for a little while and which had a voracious appetite. I made a fair " bag," and took my flies to the bat. With a pair of forceps

I held a bluebottle towards it. It raised its head, its little ears trembled, its nostrils quivered, and it made a sudden fierce lunge at the insect, grabbing it and munching it up like a dog gnawing a bone.

By the way, in spite of the country title of "flittermouse," no bat has anything to do with the rodents, for bats belong to a distinct and highly specialized order of mammals.

My bat managed the fly very well, and this notwithstanding the unusual attitude in which it dined. If you watch bats carefully as they fly through the dusk, you will often see them take queer little tumbles, falling a foot or two before righting themselves and flying on. This happens when they have made a capture and are pouching it. In the bat the tail and wings are connected by a skinny membrane, so that when the bat is on the wing and brings its tail forward beneath it, it has a bag, otherwise the interfemoral pouch, which is most useful when dealing with unruly insects. When a capture is effected, the bat bobs its head down and into the pouch, at which instant we see it fall through the air, but as it tumbles it is giving the quietus to the fly, moth, or whatever it has grabbed.

I have seen a pipistrelle try to pouch a fly presented to it while sitting on a flat surface, with the result that it fell over on its back, but it righted itself and did the trick next time. Some bats can manage to dine quite comfortably in a sitting posture, notably the long-eared bat, which will take the big quarry home to its den and deal with them at leisure. A long-eared bat that used to dwell in the rafters of the roof of a small shed, nightly littered the floor with the wings of its victims, those of moths being a conspicuous feature—yellow, orange, brown and grey, they lay in a heap and told of twilight revels.

My pipistrelle munched up another fly, and a third, when among my "bag" I found a small grey bee, an individual of one of the solitary species, and without thinking I passed it along. The bee had been badly pinched, it had little buzz left in it, but as I presented it

the bat shuddered and drew back.   Trembling, it dropped
its head and shuffled yet farther into its corner, seeming
to be in mortal fear of the bee, nor would it look at any
other insect I placed before it.

If, as it seemed, it sensed that this was a dangerous
kind of fly, it may be asked how it knew what it was ?
Bees have usually gone home before bats are abroad,
but wasps fly late at times, and maybe experience is gained
with them.   The sting of a wasp or bee would be no
light matter to so small an animal, possibly even fatal
in its consequences.

Returning to my wee sprite, I wanted to take a photograph of it, but at this it was galvanized to extreme activity.
Its whole body quivered with energy, it spread its delicate
membraneous wings—" membraneous " is a word that
expresses the transparent thinness of their texture better
than the bald English of " skinny "—and tried to take
flight.   It was no easy task to restrain it for a brief moment.
Its little jaws worked as if it was gibbering with excitement,
but no sounds were audible to my dull human ears.   It ran
this way and that, and again tried to fly off.   But I put
it back in its box, for it was better that it should wait for
evening before departing to seek a new home, though
it would not have been handicapped by the sunshine.
Bats can find their way well in a bright light, and
I remember once on a Christmas Day of exceptional
mildness, when the sun shone quite warmly, seeing a
long-eared bat hawking for insects at midday.

The nature of their food compels our bats to hibernate
during cold periods.   Most of them sleep profoundly
for the greater part of the Winter, but the pipistrelle
slumbers comparatively lightly, and is easily aroused by a
rise in temperature.   A warm evening usually brings the
flittermice from their hiding places, to race and chase
after the gnats that likewise come out when the air becomes
mild.

But about my bat.   That evening, when the sun had
vanished as an orange ball dropping behind the grey-blue
hills of the north-west, when the blackbirds were flying
off to their roosting places and the starling families were

murmuring in the shrubbery, I placed the box on a window-sill and lifted its lid.

The last house-martin swooped past, and then flew up to join its young ones which were twittering sleepily in their nest beneath the eaves, and I returned my glance to the box to see what preparations the bat was making for departure—it had gone !

The magic hour of the bats had come, and my elf of the shadows had departed.   I peered forth into the twilight and saw a little form flicker past—the bat ? I do not know ; the dusk was deepening fast ; it was a time of whispering wings and wee mysterious sounds, and the little brown elf had joined its kind.

STORIES IN STONES

By M. LOVETT TURNER

EVERY stone worked by the hand of man is an open page in the great history book of England. The gradual unfolding of everyday life is not to be seen in isolated architectural show-pieces where tourists forgather, but in the more familiar buildings that abound in small towns and country villages. Monoliths and pagan temples give way to ornate villas and military strongholds erected by our Roman colonizers. Saxon preaching crosses mingle with the butter crosses and market halls necessary to the well-being of trade, so ably fostered by those most practical of monarchs, the Tudors. Toll gates and lock-ups show how local authorities attempted to cope with increasing finance, and its attendant evils—drunkenness and robbery, while through all its pages, rivers and roads move slowly under the bridges and aqueducts that prove man's supremacy over nature herself.

Even before the mighty temples of Stonehenge and Avebury were built, man made himself a bridge. The opposite side of the river would, to his hungry mind, contain far more appetizing food than the one on which his primitive hut was built. A convenient tree trunk, hewn so that it fell across the stream, would be sufficient for the passage of the hunter but, when it became necessary to remove his cattle and the worldly possessions that will accumulate even round the most simple life, something less hazardous was needed. Early man soon found that large, flat stones placed on piers or heaps of stones, like the " clapper " bridges on Dartmoor, formed a practical and durable bridge. Tarr Steps, that famous prehistoric bridge on Exmoor, is an example of man's first engineering feat. It consists of seventeen blocks of stone, each about seven feet long and three and a half feet wide, resting on piers capable of holding their weight—a tremendous undertaking for a people who had neither suitable tools, nor mechanical means to haul and place the huge stones into position.

THE MARKET CROSS, CHICHESTER

Bridges were an asset in times of war. Is there a schoolboy who does not thrill when reading of brave Horatius and his heroic stand on Pons Sublicus, the keeping of which was in his hands? Many of our provincial bridges were, of necessity, fortified when civil war threatened, though the fortifications have long since disappeared. Monmouth, that Welsh-English town on the border that resisted practically all the Saxon kings of Wessex, Mercia and England, as well as the Danes and the Normans, before being finally subdued by William Fitzosborne, has a grim gateway standing on its bridge over the River Monnow. Although not one of the fortified gates built in Fitzosborne's time, it was quite capable of hindering the progress of an invading army, so massive are its foundations.

Many of our bridges were built and kept in repair by the Church, or monastic foundation in the neighbourhood. Penitents and public-spirited persons were persuaded to give alms, or leave money in their wills for this purpose. An old dictum that must have influenced many in this practical benevolence says, " Of all the workys in this world that ever were wrought Holy Churche is chefe, another blesseid business is brigges to make." This may account for the tiny chapels often built on the " blesseid brigge " itself. They served the dual purpose of reminding the wayfarer to pray for the soul of the builder, as well as give alms for its upkeep. Unfortunately, few bridges to-day have retained their chapels, although Wakefield, St. Ives in Huntingdonshire, Rotherham, and Bradford-on-Avon can boast of having preserved theirs. Originally the bridge at Bradford-on-Avon was built for foot passengers only, vehicles having to cross the river by the " broad ford," from which the town gets its name. Aubrey, writing in the sixteenth century, described it then as a " strong, handsome bridge, with a chapel for Masses." In the unromantic days of last century the chapel was used as an ammunition dump for the local volunteers. Previous to that it had been utilized as the lock-up for disorderly persons—quite a study in retrogression ! A curious weather vane in the form of a fish gave rise to the saying that the reveller had spent the night " under the fish and over the water," a worthy example of British humour that laughs at misfortune.

It was a decided step forward when bridges were first made of iron and steel, and many an engineer gained fame by the bridges he built. The suspension bridge, erected by Thomas Telford in 1818, and the Britannia Bridge, designed and built by Robert Stephenson in 1850, both span the Menai Straits. Brunel's great bridge, built in 1859, connecting Devon and Cornwall at Saltash, holds its own even against such giants as the bridges of the River Tay and the Firth of Forth. The latter was opened in 1890, and has a total length of a mile and a half. Over twenty acres of its surface is covered with paint—a task that must have enriched the paint trade, if nothing else. With its open girders and graceful outline, this bridge is one of the most beautiful of our many lovely bridges that have developed from the simple tree trunk of pre-historic days.

Crosses

With the spreading of Christianity stones acquired a further significance. Stone built churches replaced the wattle and daub buildings in which the earliest Christians worshipped, and stone crosses were erected wherever the work of Christ was established. Preaching crosses originated about the seventh century, and several Saxon examples, shorn of their crosspieces, but with the intricate interlaced and knot-work carving still extant, are still to be seen. The bases and shafts of two stand side by side in friendly rivalry at Sandbach, in Cheshire. Fanatics may have destroyed the cross-bars and time weathered their bases, but the carving remains to show the skill of those early masons.

Norman crosses are rare, probably due to the Normans themselves who loved to build strong, mighty works, and despised the smaller things of everyday life. The fourteenth century was prolific in crosses, but few remain intact. The Puritans have had to bear no small blame for the destruction of many of our Christian symbols,

THE CHAPEL ON THE BRIDGE, BRADFORD-ON-AVON

but often the mutilations were caused by the misguided zeal of the reformers during the ecclesiastical war with Rome, brought to a head during the reign of our Bluebeard King, Henry VIII. Why they attacked the earlier crosses that bore little more than a carved head at the apex, and left the later ones practically unharmed, is strange, for the fifteenth century crosses were crowded with figures and Calvaries—perhaps, like so many reformers of the present day, they despised the old works and respected the modern.

From the steps of the preaching cross, missionary and wandering friar spoke to the people of a heavenly home in contrast to the hovels in which they lived. Beneath its shadow rough justice was meted out to the wrongdoer showing little of Christian charity. Vagrants of either sex were ordered to be tied to the cart's tail, and whipped through the town for not having a home of their own. Ears were cut off, noses slit and bodies branded for little more than stealing a loaf of bread, or criticizing the

MONNOW BRIDGE GATEWAY, MONMOUTH

Government. Witches were tortured, and the dishonest ale-wife dragged from the steps of the cross to be ducked in the village pond for brewing bad ale.

The cross regained its dignity when used as a civic centre, standing undismayed by proclamation of king or pretender, the repealing of old laws or the reading of new ones. News of distant wars, or orders when invasion threatened, were read to the anxious crowds gathered round its base, for the cross early became the centre of village life.

Market Crosses

It was during the prosperity brought to England by the wool trade, so practically fostered by Queen Elizabeth, that the market cross, or butter cross as it was affectionately called, came to be built in many of our market towns. These miniature market halls consisted of a central shaft surrounded by steps, with a substantial roof supported on open arches. On its steps the country woman could spread her butter and eggs, and its shelter allowed the local tax gatherer to open the sacks of grain and take his toll without interference from the winds that delighted to scatter it in all directions.

Butter crosses are fairly numerous in our smaller market towns. They are usually placed in the centre of the wide street or open space where the market was held. Chichester, as befits a cathedral city that once boasted of being the military headquarters of Flavius Vespasian after the Romans had successfully colonized Britain, has a magnificent market cross. It was built by Bishop Storey in the reign of Henry VIII, to enable the cottagers to sell their home-made produce without the burden of paying market dues. The eight flying buttresses rise from the arches which form an octagonal space beneath. The twentieth century clock is somewhat of an anachronism, but must be a boon to the busy housewife.

A more honest-to-goodness butter cross stands neglected by the tourist at Cheddar, in Somerset. The richly carved apex of the cross is practically hidden by the serviceable colonnade which was added in the reign of Henry VII, when trade was beginning to flourish and the Wars of the Roses had been forgotten. Why this innovation should have been complicated by making six arches fit the octagonal steps is not clear—did the builders enjoy solving a serious mathematical problem, or was it just a mistake ?

When business was over the country folk were free to enjoy all the fun of the market. And what fun there was ! The groans of witch or heretic condemned to be burnt at the stake mingled with the crackling of the fire, or the screams of the wretch tied to the whipping post. The pillory might be occupied by a political back-slider, or pamphleteer like Daniel Defoe, who was sentenced to be placed in the pillory on three different days in seventeen, his only sin having been the publishing of a pamphlet called *The Shortest Way with the Dissenters*. The local drunkard, securely gripped by his legs in the stocks, would cause much merriment, especially when a rotten egg or decaying vegetable, cheerfully flung by an onlooker, found its mark on the unfortunate victim's face. The ungainly bear danced for the laughter lover, while cock fighting in a nearby inn, and the baiting of bulls in the bull ring, were waiting for the sporting man. Bull baiting was considered not only a sport, but a necessity. A byelaw passed in 1690 at Barnstaple ordered that no bull should be slaughtered until it had been " beaten or chased with dogs for the space of one hour, in the bull ring," for only by this inhuman method was beef considered fit to eat. Is the time-honoured custom of beating a rump steak before cooking a survival of the bull baiting so beloved by our ancestors ?

Fairs

It was round the market cross that the annual fair gathered. This was the great event of the trading year, for it benefited both the merchant and the populace. Although many of the charters granting permission to hold a fair only date from Norman days, fairs were in existence long before that. The Church's wise decision to change pagan festivals into Christian holy days attracted large numbers of churchgoers to the town on the church's patronal festival and, when mass had been duly celebrated, the worshippers were free to enjoy themselves as they wished. Marketing was brisk, and booths and amusements all added to the jollity with which fair-day was associated. The fair at Helston, in Cornwall, has its origin traced to Roman days. Alfred the Great, the benefactor of the common people, founded many fairs and markets in his kingdom, a custom that was followed by many of the monarchs that followed him. The " pole " fair at Corby, in Northamptonshire, owes its charter to Queen Elizabeth, and an interesting story is told about its origin. When this spritely queen was staying with Sir Christopher Hatton at Kirby Hall, she was rescued by some local men from a bog in which her horse had thrown her. To show her gratitude, which she was ever ready to do when it cost her nothing, she granted a charter to the villagers, exempting them from various tolls, and

FIFTEENTH CENTURY CROSS IN A PEACEFUL CORNER OF THE
CHURCHYARD, LOXTON, SOMERSET

also from attendance at the local assizes. The pole fair has grown from the custom of celebrating this privilege, and is held every twenty years. Its name is derived from the unpleasant practice of barricading the streets leading to the village and demanding toll from the traveller. If he refuses to pay, he is hoisted on a pole and carried to the village stocks and given another chance to pay, if this is refused he is then placed in the undignified position of having his feet thrust through the stocks and left to the mercy of the crowd. Needless to say, few refuse to pay the toll !

When merchants were limited to trading in one town only, the opening ceremony of the fair was often accompanied by the carrying of a large glove as a sign that the town was open to all who cared to come and sell or buy. At Exeter this glove was carried in procession and placed on the Guildhall, after which the fair was declared to be officially open. It has been suggested that this custom arose from Saxon times, when permission to hold a fair or market had to be obtained from the king, who sent one of his gloves to signify his assent.

One regrets the passing of the mop fairs, or hiring fairs, which have mostly been ousted by the dreary surroundings of the unemployment exchange. How pleasant it must have been to walk round the fair ground and see the shepherd with his crook or tuft of wool fixed in his hat, or the labourer carrying a bundle of straw, the carter with his whip, and the maid servant with her mop, or broom, all ready to start work on the morrow ? When hired these picturesque labourers were given a "fastpenny" or earnest money, which they spent on ribbons with which to deck themselves, and enjoyed their freedom for the rest of the day.

Market Halls

As trade increased and the merchant throve, market crosses were replaced by the market hall. The right to hold a market was one of the town's most treasured possessions, and was granted direct from the Crown or a religious foundation in the district, or from the lord of the manor on whose land it was held. Abington, or

Abbot's Town, in Berkshire, received its charter from the Abbot in the seventh century. Its town hall was built in the days of Charles II. Although not directly associated with Inigo Jones, this dignified building shows all the attractive features of the classical work so charmingly portrayed in his work.

Market halls followed the plan of the market cross, having open arches " under which the poor market folk could stand dry when rain cometh," as Leyland sympathetically explains—presumably he had experienced the typical weather of market days in a country town ! The toll booth in which the weights and measures were kept was on one side of the market hall, while the large upper room was where the merchants gathered to discuss their business. If the town did not possess a moot, or court room of its own, this room served its purpose, and justice was administered there by reputable burgesses. Local craftsmen, if sufficiently numerous, had their own guild halls where they met to discuss the ways and means of safeguarding their craft, and, if we dare to make such a suggestion, to finish the day with banquets and feastings !

Marketing in the Middle Ages was not merely a question of taking one's produce to the town and selling it. The woollen trade especially was hedged around with so many laws and byelaws, that they make our import and customs duties seem child's play in comparison. Wool had to be transported during the hours of daylight, and shipped from one specialized " staple " town to certain towns on the Continent. The wool sacks were examined to see that in packing they had not been " squeesed by Skrues, Press, or other Engines," or that they did not contain any " Caly, Lead, Stones, Tails, deceitful Locks, Cots, Calls, Combe or Lambswool." Evidently all these poetical intruders could be included if the wool were sold by " Tale, or number of Fleeses."

The seventeenth century produced a large number of market halls due to the prosperity of the wool trade, then at its height. The one at Ledbury, in Herefordshire, was built by John Abel in 1633. It is an imposing half-

I

OLD TURNPIKE HOUSE, STANTON DREW, SOMERSET

timbered building with sturdy pillars supporting the large upper room, and a spacious arcade beneath. The lovely octagonal market hall at Wymondham, in Norfolk, built in 1618, has an imposing staircase on the outside, with its roof gracefully tapering to a point. It looks as if it would provide little shelter for the market folk to stand dry and warm when the biting east winds blow—and only those who live near know what that means, for it is both small and high, as well as being open on all sides.

Dunster, that tiny village of Somerset so beloved by tourists and photographers, has perhaps the most picturesque market hall in England. It is known as the Yarn Market, and was built in 1600 by George Luttrel when "Dunsters" was a name that stood for all that was reliable in the yarn marketing world. Its eight gabled windows fit snugly to the roof that shelters the floor beneath. Oak beams radiate from the central pillar, one being proudly pointed out by the local inhabitants as

VILLAGE LOCK-UP, CASTLE CARY, SOMERSET

bearing the mark of a cannon ball fired during the Civil War, when Dunster Castle was held first by Parliament and then for the King. A mutilated butter cross stands a little way off, though few think to look at it.

Round Houses

Prosperity brought with it that bane of civilization, drunkenness. The tiny round houses, or lock-ups, still to be seen in many of our villages, were built in order to cope with this evil. They were not intended to be prisons as their name implies, but merely a place of security where the unruly roisterer could be safely housed until he were more amenable. More important prisoners, like highwaymen or murderers, could be kept there safely under lock and key until they could be taken to the nearest town where judgment, of a sort, was administered. There were no " Black Marias " in those days, so the malefactor might even have to spend a few days in the round house. If he died of starvation or exposure, no one was to blame—besides, he was only a prisoner, so what did it matter ?

Occasionally the round houses took their part in the country's upheavals. The lock-up at Pensford Green in Somerset, is reputed to have housed the misguided supporters of the Duke of Monmouth after his tragic defeat at Sedgemoor. On the other hand, the lock-up at Castle Cary, also in Somerset, was used as late as 1785 to confine children over the age of seven who were found playing truant from school, or breaking the Sabbath day. As school hours were from 8 a.m. to 7.30 p.m., a few hours spent in durance vile must have seemed little punishment for half a day's freedom in the fields and meadows !

The round houses were nothing if not secure. Many of the walls were two or three feet thick and the doors of studded oak. Ventilation relied on cracks in the roof or a few holes cut in the door. These also served the purpose of the prisoner's friends passing the stem of a churchwarden's clay pipe through them and, when it was safely fixed in his mouth, pouring his favourite drink into the bowl—which would not be milk we may be sure !

Drunkenness increased during the reign of Queen Anne, when the poorer classes started to drink gin. In 1714 two million gallons were distilled in England, but by 1735 this total had increased to over five million gallons. Robbery with violence and other crimes also increased, and the parish beadle, like Mr. Bumble who claimed the honour of having named Oliver Twist, had charge of the keys and was responsible for the good behaviour of the village. Charles I who, in spite of his many amorous occupations, was extremely practical and had the well-being of his country at heart, inaugurated a band of men—nicknamed Charlies from their royal patron—to keep order in the city. Like the parish beadle, these early policemen were more often missing than present when trouble came. It was due to the untiring efforts of Henry Fielding, the novelist, that our towns and villages were eventually safeguarded. He was a magistrate at Bow Street Court, noted for never having received a bribe, and after lengthy discussions was granted permission to start his band of Bow Street Runners, as they were called. The number at first was only seventeen, but so efficient did they become that the cry of " the Scarlet Runners " was sufficient to clear the streets and quell any disturbance.

One by one the village lock-ups and stocks have disappeared and been replaced by the more humdrum police station. The parish beadle has merged into the friendly policeman, and our villages have little to show of those troublesome days when walking abroad in the dark was both a dangerous and hair-raising experience.

Toll Gates and Turnpikes

Travelling, even in the light of day, was a hazardous proceeding. Roads were mostly ill-defined trackways, axle deep in mud and, if the farmer's land spread on both sides of the road, he simply ploughed over it, leaving the unfortunate wayfarer to find his own path over the furrows. Had the splendid roads made by the Romans been kept in repair, the history of our country might have been different. It is said that Cromwell captured nine hundred Royalist horses that had stuck in the mud and been abandoned. Even as late as the eighteenth century

Daniel Defoe tells of a devout lady who was driven to church behind a team of six oxen—and not one too many if his description of the roads were true. Foot passengers, and even horsemen, were known to lose the pathway and be drowned in the ditches on the side of the road. Half-hearted attempts had been made from time to time to mend the main roads. A law passed in the reign of Queen Elizabeth ordered that the wheels of heavy waggons must be at least nine inches wide to flatten out the ruts made by lighter vehicles.

Toll was levied on the road between London and York in the seventeenth century, but as the money was rarely used for repair work, little improvement was effected. It was due to the fashionable foible of the wealthy, who decided to follow the custom of Queen Anne and spend their leisure at our inland spas, that the work of keeping the roads fit for travellers was seriously taken in hand. Beau Nash, the uncrowned king of Bath, raised the large sum of £1,800 to mend the roads leading to his beloved city, but it was either misspent or insufficient, judging by the complaints of its visitors for many years afterwards.

In 1727 the first practical scheme for the betterment of the highway was adopted, and turnpike trusts were established to collect tolls. Toll houses were built and toll gates fixed at the entrances to the towns and villages—an innovation that invited the adventurous youth to rush his horse at the gate and leap over, waving a cheery farewell to the outraged gate keeper. Field paths became popular, or one man might keep the attention of the keeper while his friends rushed through the gates, leaving him alone and gaping without the tolls that were his due.

In the beginning of the nineteenth century, when each road had its toll gate fixed every few miles, gangs of roughs spread terror in the heart of every toll keeper. Calling themselves Rebekahites, an ungainly word based on the Biblical blessing bestowed on Rebekah which ran, " Let thy seed possess the gates of them that hate thee," they disguised themselves in white garments with masks over their faces. The unfortunate gate keeper was roused

from his bed with hideous blasts on a cow horn. Then
the toll house, often a charming little residence with
windows that faced up and down the road, was either
burnt to the ground, or the gates destroyed and the roof
taken off.

Fortunately for the peace of the countryside, but
unfortunately for the victim, an old woman of seventy
was shot dead for calling out that she knew the names
of her persecutors. The coroner's jury, either being
Rebekahites themselves or having been bribed by them,
brought in a verdict that the deceased " had died from
an effusion of blood into the chest, which occasioned
suffocation ; but from what cause is to the jury unknown."
This preposterous verdict caused such a stir that a commission was set up to enquire into the alleged hardships
entailed by the levying of tolls, and they gradually
disappeared, leaving only a few private roads and bridges
where toll was demanded. The little toll houses became
private houses and the gates disappeared, leaving only
the iron hasps to tell of the days when a visit to the market
town was quite an expensive outing.

Tolls were demanded for practically everything. A
table drawn up in 1881, and still standing by the toll gate
at Tucton Bridge, gives an entertaining list of tolls. This
includes the stage coach, landau, barouche, phaeton,
chaise, hearse, and other delights of our grandparents.
The motor-car was unknown, but any person riding a
horse or beast is included—perhaps to catch anyone who
followed the example of Jonathon Thatcher, who rode his
cow to market in order to avoid paying the horse tax
imposed by Pitt in 1784. Heavy vehicles were charged
by weight, and weighing machines were often placed
at the side of the toll house. A particularly imposing
one is to be seen at Soham, in Cambridgeshire, which
looks like a second cousin to a windmill, with its over-
lapping boards and uncouth collection of chains and posts.
Few to-day think of it as a relic of the days when the
wayfarer had to pay toll for the benefit of using the king's
highway.

The office of toll keeper was eagerly sought, for it was

both an easy and lucrative occupation in spite of its many drawbacks. The little toll gate house at Sark, in Dumfriesshire, must have been a veritable goldmine to the keeper, for it is the first building over the border from Carlisle and a serious rival to the famous Gretna Green smithy. In its "marriage room" over 10,000 couples have been united since it was built in 1830. Perhaps it was of such a toll house that Sam Weller, senior, thought when he said he would quit the cheery life of driving the stage coach and "keep a pike" in order to avenge his wrongs on the travellers who had annoyed him !

OLD YARN MARKET, DUNSTER

THE
DALESWOMAN'S TALE

By H. J. Scott

We are inclined to think of unusual beliefs as something unworthy of a rational being, and, even when we half accept them, we pretend to treat them as little more than a nursery game. We deride them even when we, secretly, carry a much travelled and extremely shrivelled broad bean in an inner pocket as a preventive of rheumatism—as I have known to be the habit of more than one shrewd public man in the North country.

A number of years ago I was present in a Yorkshire home when the daughter of the house returned from a visit to the dentist. Scarcely was she in the house before she produced the errant tooth which the dentist had removed, and, with great ceremony, it was covered with salt, wrapped in a small piece of brown paper, and solemnly cast into the fire. There was much surprise when I inquired the significance of the rite.

" Eh, don't thee know ? I reckon we'd have no luck this year if we didn't make sure yon tooth were burnt. Don't thee do that wi' thy teeth ? We're not what thee might call superstitious like, but tha cannot be too careful about serious things, tha knows."

There are few counties which can boast a richer traditional store of curious beliefs and—what is more strange—where so many of those beliefs are still so strongly, if secretly, held. In the county of the broad acres, where the hills rise to cloud level and the dales are honeycombed with eerie pot-holes that go down hundreds of feet into the earth—a county that has depth as well as breadth and height—there is an external native shrewd-ness and a quality of dourness which often hides a vein of belief in the supernatural and the unseen. They have a saying in the North concerning the stranger that you must " Summer him and Winter him before you trust him," and it is a good test in those bleak fell lands where the very trees are bowed in the back by Winter's storms, and where it takes long years to win an " intake " back from the moors into cultivation. Only after such a test does the " off-coomed un " cease to be a " foreigner," and win admission to those inner depths where he learns of " barguests " and " trolls " and " boggarts " and other inhabitants of the unseen world.

After many years of living in one of the remoter valleys of Yorkshire, I had walked over from my valley into the next dale to call on a farmer friend, and it was com-forting to drop down out of the wind which blew keen and chill on the tops of the limestone fells into the blue shadows and quiet peace of the dale, and to descend from the bleak heights where only the curlews and lapwings called to the friendly bird songs of the lowland. It was still better to step into the warm farm kitchen and sit in great content beside the cheery blaze of a fire that reached halfway up the chimney. My farmer friend was out when I arrived, but his wife invited me in and promptly poked up the fire under the kettle.

"Thou mun have a cup o' tea while tha waits," she said. "Jim'll be in, I reckon, in two-three minutes. Sit thisen down."

So I toasted my toes at the great arched fireplace, with its vast oven and its side boiler where the water is always hot. I gazed at the two china dogs beside the mantelpiece, at the twinkling brass candlestick, and at the great bellows hanging on the wall. And I felt the deep content that was somehow as characteristic of this Yorkshire farmhouse as its weathered stone porch and its thick three-centuries-old walls. There is no peace on earth so profound as that which descends upon a North country farmhouse kitchen in the lull between the midday meal and teatime.

As that farmer's wife and I talked by the fireside, her gnarled and busy fingers went on knitting ceaselessly, as they had probably done in every spare moment for over half a century. She was an elderly woman, with hair which had been only iron-grey when I knew her first, but which now was almost snow-white and contrasted rather oddly with her brown, weather-beaten, time-worn face. Yet her features were well-shaped and had been, I believe, very handsome, though perhaps never beautiful.

Quite how our talk took the turn it did I cannot recall. I think it began when she lamented that one of the cows, which with sheep were the mainstay of this typical Yorkshire hill farm of the dales country, had just produced another bull-calf, the third running, and that her husband had been justly angry about it.

"I telled him," she said, "that it was his own fault. He should 'a let me feed 'un. But he wouldn't have it."

"How would that have saved the situation?" I asked.

"Don't thee know the old dales way of it?" she answered. "If t'woman of t'house doesn't feed t'cow what's going to calve, then that cow'll allus give bull calves."

From that I discovered that underneath all her traditional native wit, and her hard practical experience of the grim ways of these Northern dales, there ran an unsuspected and powerful belief in an unseen power expressed in a multitude of signs and wonders.

She talked of strange events in the lives of the men and women of the little dale, many of whom had long turned to dust and whose names are chiselled on the stones in the tiny church cemetery. Her mind teemed with memories of people and events, not all tragical in character, yet in all of them she saw the work of some unseen hand; evidence of the supernatural world she so profoundly believed in. Even if I had been in no mood for listening, her eyes would have held me. Her fiercely pleading gaze cast a spell which held me as firmly as the sincerity in her voice.

The spell was at last broken abruptly when my farmer friend came in, for he was a tall, raw-boned dalesman, with a practical mind that had little room for other things than sheep and cows and crops, and the everyday happenings of the dale. His wife's talk gradually slipped out of mind as I sipped my hot tea and fed his old sheep-dog with a few crumbs and bits of broken biscuit from my pocket, and enquired how things were with him.

" Nowt much different," he declared. " Things don't alter much in this part. There was a shoot last week. Aye, and I sold four gimmers yesterday. Fine gimmers they were, too. Oh, and ye remember old Tom Armthwaite—t'blacksmith on t'Green ? " he asked.

" Wasn't he the man who lost his leg in the last war ? " I queried.

" Aye, that's him. Well, 'e died about a month back. And then there was Mrs. Marley, from t'Post Office. 'Appen ye didn't know 'er. She went last Tuesday. Poor woman, she'd 'ad a lot o' suffering."

" Yes, I remember her," I said. " She used to make doughnuts and toffee, I think ? "

" That's 'er. Well, she's gone," he said. " That's two o' t'old uns."

" And now we're waiting," said his wife, without looking up from her resumed knitting.

I think I looked surprised. " Waiting ? What for ? " I asked.

"For t'third," she answered in a steady, even voice.

My farmer friend looked up apologetically, with a suspicion of a smile on his face. He moved to the door, with a gesture of impatience. "Like to see t'pigs I bought t'other week?" he invited. "They're a grand lot."

By this time he had reached for his hat and his pipe, and was at the door waiting for me.

"Come on, Jess," he called to his dog, and out we went to inspect the pigs.

It was a month or more before I climbed over those high tops again to the warm shelter and calm of that remote dale. By then the chill winds of Autumn had given place to the heavy stillness of early snows. A white blanket had covered the familiar limestone escarpments and had given them a new and softer aspect. The crumbling dry-stone walls, that look like a grey net thrown over the landscape, had been transformed into lines of wool that could be distinguished from the general whiteness only by the shadows they threw. Many sheep had been overblown and buried in the drifts, which in places were a dozen feet deep. I met my farmer friend crossing the old high road over the fell. He had been out with his dog since daybreak rounding up scattered sheep and probing the likely drifts for any that were in danger of being smothered.

"Four out so far," he said wearily. "But I reckon there may be as many more beneath this lot. Thee'd better go on down to t'farm, and I'll be down in a bit when I've worked up yon wall-side. There's sure to be one or two there."

I offered to go with him, but he wouldn't have it.

"No need for two on us to get soaked," he said. "Besides," he added, "t'missus would like to see ye."

He whistled up his dog, and strode off towards a sheer white precipice of snow under which his sheep might have sought shelter.

"Have ye seen Jim?" asked his wife, when at last I stumbled down to the old farmhouse. "Then he'll 'a told ye. That poor old Mrs. Mason from t'public died a fortnight ago."

There was something in the flourish with which she moved the kettle on to the fire, and poured out the inevitable cup of tea, that betokened her satisfaction. It was unlikely, I thought, as I watched her pick up her knitting and settle down in the armchair by the fire, that she would not return to the topic of my last visit.

" I hope ye don't think I'm crowing over ye," she said suddenly after a pause, " but I reckon ye doubted my word when I told ye it's ill done to go against accepted things, for when Providence gives us signs and omens like as for our guidance, yans a girt fool to go against 'em."

" But I don't understand why———— "

" Aye, there ye're right," she broke in, almost gleefully, and with that intense look in her eyes.   " Ye don't understand.   I reckon there are lots o' folk who at some time or other in their lives happen on something they doesn't understand or which they say is unbelievable.   But it happens—that's t'thing that beats 'em."

She glanced up at the ancient clock on the mantelpiece, and asked me unexpectedly where Jim was.

" He was going to work up the long wall on High Fell before he came down," I replied.

" Then he'll be a bit yet," she said.   " Listen, and I tell ye a story.   Jim 'ud laugh.   He always does laugh, but if ye don't mind an old woman's tale I reckon ye might be interested.   And it might help ye to understand," she added.

If I had declined the honour I think she would still have got her story in, but in that warm kitchen, with the firelight twinkling on the shining brasses and casting a mellow glow over the old beams that carried their drying hams and bunches of seasoning, I was in no mood to refuse her.   Truth to tell, that now familiar intensity of her voice and manner carried greater conviction than I can describe.   She raked some peats on to the fire, gathered her old shawl more closely about her shoulders, and after fumbling for a moment over the resumption of her knitting, began a recital which I shall always remember as one of the oddest of my experiences.

" It was an early Winter like this many years ago when it happened, and it was in a dale not very far from this.

There were a young lass name of ——, but there's no need to tell ye t'name. She hadn't been wed much more than a year and were expecting her first. T'place where she was living was a lonely enough spot, one of a couple o' farm cottages at end o't'dale, and what made it worse was that her husband had only been taken off to t'hospital a few days before. T'doctor wanted her to go off to hospital seeing how things were, but when she found it wouldn't be t'same hospital as her man, she wouldn't go. She made up her mind that t'child ought to be born at home, and that her husband 'ud like it so. She were stubborn about it.

"Not that she weren't nervous about it, too. There was only an old woman in t'next cottage to give her a hand, and when t'doctor were leaving her near her time she clutched his arm tight and said huskily, ' Tha'll come, doctor, won't thee ? Soon as they send for thee tha'll come.'

" ' Of course,' said t'doctor.

"But she won't take that for an answer. ' Swear tha'll come whatever happens,' she said.

" T'doctor—he were a youngish chap—was a bit put out by her insistence, and he didn't fairly like to have his word doubted that way, but reckoning to humour her, took her by t'hand and said gravely, ' Yes, I swear I'll come.'

" T'poor lass were greatly relieved and even waved to him, light-heartedly like, as she watched him go down to t'little garden gate, carefully fasten t'sneck, and follow t'snow-covered path down to where t'old road along t'dale began. It was a grey day with a bit o' snow falling, and t'top o' t'fells that shut in t'dale were hidden in mist. Before night it were snowing hard. There was a fair blizzard raging, but t'lass felt content wi' her promise, and t'doctor knew she'd be all right for a day or two, although he told his old housekeeper that he were right glad he'd got up to t'dale head when he had ; it made t'girl feel more comfortable and set his mind at rest.

"Well, it snowed all that night and t'best part o' t'next day, and about ten at night t'doctor looked out o' t'window and saw that although t'blizzard had gone there was still a sight o' snow falling. ' I reckon there'll be no call to-night,' he said to himself, as he put out t'lights and went to bed. 'But I must go up to t'dale head in t'morning. Queer, that lass making me swear to come like that.'

" It would be about two in t'morning that t'doctor were wakened by somebody ringing his doorbell like mad, and I reckon he swore a bit as he went to his window and looked out.

" ' Who is it ? ' he asked.

" ' This is me, Kit Calvery, shepherd fra Bickersdale,' said t'caller. ' Her at t'dale head's been taken bad. She's 'ad a fall and ye're wanted quick. I'd go back wi' ye, but I'm fair done in. I'll knock up Seth Whitehouse though. He'll go wi' ye.'

" ' No, no,' said t'doctor. ' I'll manage.'

" ' It's a bad neet, doctor, wi' big drifts. Tha'd best have someone. T'road's bad as owt.'

" But t'doctor wouldn't listen to him nor to his old housekeeper, who'd been wakened by all t'noise, and who wanted him to call up a man nearby who did odd jobs for him so that there'd be two on 'em. He said he knew t'way all right and, anyway, would take a lantern, then he could follow t'shepherd's footprints. And in a few minutes he'd set off.

" T'snow had stopped falling by then but it were pitch black, for there were no moon and there was a blanket of snow still in t'sky. His lantern showed him t'shepherd's tracks but no more, and it took him longer than he thought to get into t'old dale road, where t'snow were wall high in places and where there were no landmarks, as ye might say, except here and there a plantation o' firs and maybe a barn or two. And even they look a sight different when they're all capped i' snow. He stumbled on, though, till he come to t'place where t'tracks left t'road to climb up t'farm, and then he all at once missed 'em in a rough patch. He searched this way and that, till suddenly he stepped on a patch of snow that gave way and he pitched right over on his face. T'lantern went out and rolled down t'slope, and he were completely lost. T'doctor said after, that t'darkness seemed like to suffocate him.

He could see no ways at all, and although he were nobbut shaken by his fall, he didn't know which way to turn. Wherever he went he seemed to sink up to his knees in t'snow and he floundered about, poor chap, like a horse that's bogged. He'd kept hold of his bag, but he couldn't find t'lantern, and yet he reckoned that unless he found it there'd be little chance for him or her. It'd be a deal of time before dawn, and then it might be too late.

" Then it was that he remembered how she'd made him swear he'd come. She'd believe he'd not fail her, that is, if she were in a fit state to remember. He must get to her somehow. And t'thought o' that made him try all t'harder to find his lantern or at least get back to t'dale road. But more he tried, more he seemed to flounder, and he could feel t'snow cold against his legs as his clothes got wet through. His hands were bleeding, too, where he'd scrubbed them against t'stones and t'walls. Though he struggled on he were thoroughly beaten.

" It were in that black moment when everything seemed hopeless that he heard what he said was like a wild bird's cry in t'silence. It were like no bird he'd ever heard, and he said it may not have been a bird at all. But t'sound of it was clear enough, and all at once he remembered an old legend o' t'dale that a big white bird was supposed to watch over all t'folk who lived thereabouts, because in far-off times someone had fed it through a bad Winter. Afore he knew rightly what he was doing he called out.

" ' Quick,' he cried, ' afore it is too late. Get me to t'cottage for t'sake o' t'mother and child.'

" For a moment or two there was no sound except a faint noise o' t'wind like a sigh. He began to laugh at himself for fool unnerved by t'snow. And then a dog barked. At first t'doctor thought he were mistaken. Then t'bark came again, close by. He set off to follow t'sound, stumbling and staggering through drifts and gullies. T'dog, he thought, must belong to one of those two cottages, and he whistled again and waited. Again he heard t'bark o' t'dog and went on. He were just fearing that he was going still further astray when his hand touched something. It was a wooden gate, and

K

he knew it was t'right one. As he put his hand down to lift t'sneck something soft and alive brushed past him and he saw t'shadow o' something. It had the shape of a dog wi' a long shaggy tail.

"It were getting daylight when, after t'mother and child were safe, he and t'old woman who had come in to help were sitting by t'kitchen fire drinking tea.

"'Where's t'dog?' said t'doctor, knowing that it was only the dog's bark that had saved t'lives of two, if not three, of them.

"'What dog?' asked t'old woman.

"'Why, t'dog that barked in t'night. It was outside when I came in.'

"She shook her head. 'There's no dog here, nor did I hear one, and I were listening for you all t'time.'

"'But I followed it here,' he said.

"'I knows of no dog this end o' t'dale,' she answered.

"And because he insisted, and because she could make nowt on it, they went out to t'gate to look. There had been no more snow, and there was a reddish glow over t'east side where t'sun were rising. Outside t'gate there were two sets o' footprints. One was t'shepherd's going down t'hill, and t'other was t'doctor's coming up. There were no sign of a dog's tracks."

The farmer's wife was a little breathless when her story ended, although she had kept up her interminable knitting during its telling, stopping only now and then to pull her shawl tighter round her old shoulders. Neither of us spoke for a full minute after it was done, and the farm kitchen, now in darkness but for the firelight, was filled with a hundred shadows with only the gentle ticking of the clock on the mantelpiece to disturb them.

"Well," she said, as I did not speak. "Do you understand now?"

"I think so," I answered, a little lamely. "But what makes you believe that to be true?"

For a moment she hesitated and then, very quietly and very slowly, answered, "Because I was t'young mother and our Fred was t'child that was born that night. I've got to believe it."

WILLIAM PLASTOW'S STORY

As told in Bucks. Dialect to

H. HARMAN

VISITOR. " I have come to ask for a few particulars about the inclosures. I hear you lived soon after they took place, and that you know more about them than anybody living in Haddenham."

MR. PLASTOW. " I waunt alive when that happund; but all I know about em was told me by mi grand-fath-ur. I also heeurd a good many old peepul speeak about em— that was when I was a boey—but they be all dead and gone; none an em be left. They took pleeace in 1831, and I was born in 1839, so I doo-ant remember the opun feeulds and the furlongs; but the incloasures wuz one a the wust things that ivver happund to Hadnum.

" If ye goo along the lower rooad as leeads from Teeam to Aiuhlsburry towards Dintun, ye ull find Hewdon farm layin an the right. Inside one a the barns thaiur's rit an a beeam, 1832—that was the deeat when the incloasures was finished and all the feeulds brought togither into big farms.

" Afuur that the common graiazin land stretched by the streeam frum Dintun to Scotsgrove and then by the side a the river past Notley Abbey, and thaiur all the freeholders had right a pasturige; they were allowed so many cattul aich to graiaze, and if anybody put moour an than what he was allowed, a man who was called a ' driver ' druv em awf. He was imployed to look arter the cattul, so he knowed how many aich man ought t'ave; but you alwiz find somebody who wants to a moour than his sheear, and that was the way aich man had ony what belonged to him. Well, all the graiazin lands were dividid up into big meddurs, some an em were Stanbridge Meead, Beeany

Meead, Middle Meead, Veeasum's Meead, Anxey Meddur, and Youlsome Meead ; tuthers I doo-ant remember now. Each a these meeads was sheeard for mowin among different people, but thaiur waunt any hedges, ur balks to mak awf what belonged to aich an em, but what they done was to mark out an the sad an opposit sides a the meead some sign sich as a trough or summut else as ood mark the boundary to ther mowin—one man marked one thing and another another, so they could alwiz tell how fur ther mowin went. The meeads were shet up in spring, and when the grass was fit they employed boeys to run frum one mark athurt the standin grass to the mark an tuther side, and the track the boey maiad showed the boundary a ther mowin ; and I a heeurd William Hutt say many a time as he was the boey as run the last path— that was jest afuur th' incloasures took pleeace.

" On Lammas day all the graiazin land become open to the freeholders, so if anybody ant got his hay up by then he ood lose it as all the cattul an that deeat were turned out to pasture, and it waunt alwiz as they got ther hay up by then, fur sometimes thaiur was a wet summer like we a had this yeeur, and then it was a bad thing for many an em.

" The arable land a the parish lay up an the high ground out a the raich a the floods and was dividid into three gret feeulds called Downhill feeuld, Dollicott feeuld, and Cott's Hill feeuld, and the three-course system was alwiz follured. One lay fallur aich yeeur. Aich a these feeulds was divided up into smaller ones, and these into the furlongs with the balks atween. Some a these smaller feeulds had some- times as many as fifteen or sixteen furlongs and some had moour, each a th' furlongs was about a aiacre, but an the whool they used to be a li-ul under. Some had perhaps forty or fifty a these furlongs, and they were pleeacd all ovur the parish. Perhaps thaiur were one or two in one feeuld neeur Dintun, five or six neeur Notley Abbey, and perhaps twenty or thurty in other parts a the parish, so it was a bit inconvainient to cultivaiat, but the people got a good livin, and they had the reward fur the wurk they put an the land. The cattul in the summer graiazed an the fallurs and an the balks, that was when the meeads were shet up fur mowin. When harvist come and the craps stood in the feeulds, aich man had to pay his tenth fur tithe. Thaiur was one shock in ivvery ten, ivvery tenth cock a barley, ivvery tenth mule a milk, ivvery tenth pig, and a tenth of anythink else that was grown an the land, but they dint taiak ivvery tenth child; I nivver heeurd as they done that, and thaiur were a good few an em in Hadnum at that time.

"Well, about 1830 some noatices were put an the church door, sayin that the feeulds were gooin to be incloased. When the news got about the village, the people went and toour (tore) em down. They were put up agen, but they toour em down agen, but it waunt no use, fur the Commissionur come down and started to incloase the feeulds. Thaiur was one man who had moour to do wi it than anybody else, as he stood to gaian a good deeul; but it waunt long afure he had a terrible affliction, and the people all su-ur it was judgmint an him. Poor thing, his dartur was helpliss all hur life, and she ant bin long dead; but we maunt judge nobody.

"Howivver, when the Commissionur startid, they were sich a long time befuur anythink was done that fur a whool yeeur the people dint know in what parts of the parish the land allottid to em was pleeaced; so that yeeur nauthing was sowed and nobody had any craps at the eend an it; neeurly ivvery small man was practically ruined. Nauthing had come in, and thaiur was the ixpense of ther families gooin an all the time. Next yeeur when they had got thaiur land, thaiur was the ixpense of quickin and incloasin it, fur the Commissionur woont give a proper titul to the incloasure if it waunt in order. An the top a this, new rooads had to be maiad and the ixpense a these all come out a the reeats, so they riz to ovur a pound in the pound. The little man coont feeace this, and so most an em went to the wall, bisides if he had any cattul he coont graiaze em now an the commun feeulds, so he found neeurly all was gone. Some took mortgages an ther land, but coont pay the interest and were sold out, and a few yeeurs laiater the price a carn fell, and most a them who had strugguld, to kaip an could kaip an no longer, and they fell out too. Some yeeurs artur the carn riz, and the few as had got ovur the terrible times got an and maiad therselves.

"These times lasted fur some yeeurs, and then come the opportunity for rich men to taiak advantage of the poour. They bought the small farms and added em to theirn, and ony imployed as many men an the whool lot as could cultivaiat one farm propurly. I heeurd one man say, 'When ye see feeuld added to feeuld an farm to farm, then it's bad fur the whool village,' and so it was, ispecially fur Hadnum, and I hope sich a time ull nivver come agen.

"It was a cryin shaiam for the hard-wurkin man to lose his land and become a laiabourer, and Hadnum was full an em artur the incloasures. Afuur thaiur were moour shephurds in the village than what thaiur are farm laiabourers at the present day. Nobody ood lend the poour man any money to help him ; then if he kep his land, how could he buy stock to dress it. Ivverything was agenst him, but it waunt agenst the man wi plenty a money. I knowed one man wi plenty who had a ai-acre a turnups, gret turnups as ivver I did see. He went to Aiuhlsburry markut and bought forty good strong ship and folded em an the feeuld. In a week he sold em fur ten shillings a piece more than what he gin fur em, bisides thaiur was another crap next year when he sowed his carn ; but how could a poour man do that ? He ant got the money to buy the ship and nobody ood lend it him. The pleeace was filled with laiabourers and they dint know wheeur to git a job. Some an em used to walk to Dintun to git a day's threshin, but if it raiand they got no money, and yit afuur the incloasures they had had ther own land. Then they did git summut fur ther laiabour, fur whativver they put in the land they got out an it and moour too, fur they did wurk hard and got a reward fur what they done. The schooulmaster at Dintun used to come ovur and spaik to the men, and then they got Joseph Arch down, and as times dint seem to improve, a good many men, and thauir were some fine strong men in Hadnum then, left the village ; some went to Lancashire and Yorkshire, bisides other pleeaces, and some went abroad.

"Well, ivverybody waunt down an em. Thaiur was ole Squire Franklin as did ivverything he could to help em as rentid lands awf him. He gin em stock and in some ceeases (cases) woont taiak any rent fur three yeeurs. If thaiur had bin moour men like him, Hadnum woont a suffered as it did."

VISITOR. "How did all these unemployed men with their families live?"

MR. PLASTOW. "They dint know what to do; they sarched ivverywhere fur imploymint, but few could git it; thaiur was gret distress and want all through the pleeace. The wust an it was thaiur waunt any allotments then; they come laiater. Some a the housen had a few pole a ground at ther back duur, but not enoh to lay by a stooar a taiaturs fur the wintur; besides, taiaturs were sceearce in them days. Some a the farmers let ther men a ten or twenty poles a ground in one a ther feeulds, and that was how they eeked out a livin; but them as were out a wurk dint a that; they had to goo wi-out, and it was ispecially bad fur em when thaiur was a hard winter. Nobody can realise what a blessing it is to have a good crap a taiaturs stoared in yur barn fur the winter, only them as a bin through hard times like they were in Hadnum artur the incloasures. When ye got em in yur barn they be yourn, and ye can goo and git em whenivver ye want em. The peepul used to a pais cooked wi whativver they got and they also used to a pai-soup. The farmers then growed a lot of pais, and they used to be sold in the shops. I a took many a looad to Aiuhlsburry to be sold in the shops. Ivverybody used to have em. When autumn come, the big cabbage as were grown in the garduns were liftid up by the roots and tied head downurds under the roof a the batn with the dirt an. Then in wintur ye used to goo and cut a bit out, jest as much as ivver ye wantid. Thaiur waunt much fresh mait fur the poour, but they had baiacon dumpling sometimes.

"A long su-ut puddun wi chopped baiacon in it mixed up wi inen. When I went to the schooul jest behind the Wesleyan Chapul, thaiur was a boey as alwiz brought a inen dumpling fur dinner; that was a big inen biled in the dumpling—some used to a them. Times be better now, and a good thing they be. I a bin a-reeadin in the paiaper as they be puttin up new housen with ony ten pole a gardun ground. That's wrong. Ivvery new house ought to a a rood a ground, then a man can git enoh to last him and his family all the yeeur round, bisides havin summut as he can sell. If at the time a the incloasures the people a Hadnum had a rood or so as they could a cultivaiated, thaiur woont a bin the distress as thaiur wur; twur the delay a the Commissionur's in not tellin the people fur a whool yeeur wheeur ther lands lay as maiad Hadnum goo to the wall.

"Ah, I lived wi mi ole grandfath-ur and grandmoth-ur. I knowed what they had suffered, and since they a bin dead, I a laid abed many a time and cried at what they went through. They a bin at rest now fur a good long while, and it wunt be long afuur I be at rest wi em, as I be eighty-seven yeeurs old and can't ixpect to live much longer. Ah! many a time in the long dark nights have I thought an em and what they done fur me; and then I think a mi past life and what I a done. Sometimes I graive and sometimes I feeul happy.

"Well, my boey, alwiz do what's right, and if ye can help it nivver do any wrong. If ye cant do nobody any good, nivver do em any harm, fur tis them people as do harm as alwiz causes sich misery in the woruld. Thaiur's one thing I always feeul I done right in, and I awfen think an it. My grandmoth-ur had brought me up from a baiaby and ceeard (cared) fur me like a mothur. They alwiz looked artur me and sheeuldid me and protectid me quite as much as if she had bin mi own peearent (parent). When I had got to be a strongish lad, I begun to think a what e was gooin to be, and I thought e would be a carpinter, fur I dint like the idea of havin to goo through what they had gone through; so I used to tell it about pritty awfen, not knowin I should a to leeav the village to git apprenticed. One day, when induurs, I mentioned it agen, and I could see by ther feeaces they were a bit concarned. So one day soon artur she says to me, 'When yur poour mothur died and left ye a baiaby, we took ye, and brought ye up and a alwiz a-treeated ye as ur own child. We a looked artur ye and ceeared for ye, and now we be a-gittin old and can't wurk, we thought ye ood stay wi us and help us in ur old age. Ye ull do wrong if ye leeav us.' All at once I thought a the sacrifice they had maiad for me all through the terrible time they had pahst, so I said, ' Granny, I ull nivver leeav ye nur fursaiak ye as long as ivver ye live.' And I nivver did. I lived wi em all ther lives and helped em all I could till they boath died, and then I laiad em to rest."

VISITOR. "When did they die ?"

MR. PLASTOW. "My grandfath-ur died in 1865 and my grandmoth-ur a few yeeurs afuur that. I alwiz feel I done right in stayin wi em, and that a bin one a the grettest satisfactions a mi life. My grandfath-ur left me the little house we lived in and about a ai-acre a ground to 't, but it was mortgaged fur moour than it was wuth. At the time a the incloasures he got about twenty ai-acres at Roundhill fur his lot. He kep sixteen and sold tuthers to pay his debts ; but the reeats fur the new rooads and the ixpenses a quickin and incloasin were too much fur him, and he coont git an. Th' overseers were always a-callin fur money ; thaiur was one ooman who was afreead whenivver she heeurd her frunt geeat opun as she thought somebody was shuur to come fur money ; she toald me that hurself. Why, they coont pay sometimes the rooadman ther weekly waiages a aiaht shillings a week ; they had to goo to somebody to git him to pay his reeats an the Saturday afuur the man could be paid— thaiur waunt no money about.

" My grandfath-ur had a lot a bad luck at that time. He had a cow die and then a horse ; so he sold one horse fur sixty pounds and put it in the bank, and another to a man fur the saiam money, but he nivver paid fur it. Soon arter the bank broke and he only got sixty half-crowns fur his sheear. So one thing comin an the top a tuther broke him and he had to give up. He got a man naimd Cross a London to buy his sixteen ai-acres fur twenty-two pounds a ai-acre, but neeurly all an it went in the reeats and ixpenses a encloasin. At the saiam time the man agreed to let my grandfath-ur have a leeas an the land at twenty-two shillins a ai-acre fur twenty-one yeeurs. As soon as the man got it he took part an it away and planted it wi trees, then he took some moour and at last all an it; and that's how my grandfath-ur was left wi ony the little cottage wi the one ai-acre attached to it.

"Ah! these men frum London as lent money an mortgage were a hard lot—they had no murcy an the poour. They got ivverything they could and took ivvery advantage, so that whoivver got in ther hands was stripped of all he got. This is the kind a men they were: Some Hadnum men borrowed some money frum one a these London men, and soon they begun to feel his tarms were a bit hard; so they went up to London to see if they could git a bit awf. They went to his shop, and when they went inside he was in it among his wurkpeople. As soon as he see the Hadnum men, he said to them around him, 'You a got some funny fellurs heeur, but I ull show ye summut wonderful.'

"He then went to speeak to the Hadnum men and said, 'I sell ivverything in my shop. I can let ye have whativver ye want.' So one an em said, 'Then sell me a bit a barley straa fur mi shoes.' That done him, fur he ant got any a that. Soon artur he says, 'Heeur's a shilling fur aich a ye.' So he give aich an em a shilling. 'Now,' says he, 'I a gin aich an ye a shilling; if ye gi me back the shilling I can gi aich an ye a half a crown.' So they give him back the shilling, but he dint give em the half a crown; so they axed him for it. 'No,' says he, 'I dint say as I ood gi it ye back, I said I *could*; but I baint a gooin to.' So they had nauthing at all. That was the kind a men the people had to deeul wi in them days.

"Well, my grandfath-ur was left at last wi ony his little cottage and a ai-acre a ground, and artur his death I got married and lived in it. I wurked as hard as any man did (and I could wurk in them days). I wurked forrad in the marnin and laiat at night, but e coont git an as the interest e had to pay an the mortgage swallured ivverything e arnt. One night a fire broke out in th' house and burnt it to the ground. We escaiaped (escaped) wi our lives, but lost ivverything ixcept a few things. The naiahbours were good; they took us in and sheltered us, and gin mi childern some clo-athes. I got a hunderd pounds frum the insurance, so I paid it to the man who hilt the mortgage, and then was left wi nauthing.

"Howivver, I found e was better off wi ony mi weekly waiages at twelve shilling a week, fur now e ant got any moour interest to pay; and so e wcnt an. I come in this heeur house arter the fire and I be in it now. Ah! I wurked hard to maiak eends meet—and I a wurked hard in mi time.

"I a fagged half a ai-acre a day many a time and arned me five shillings—I was at it at fuur o'clock in the marnin till laiat at night. I wurked fur mi mahster fur thurty yeeurs, and alwiz sarved him faithfully. I alwiz done ivverything e could and done the very best fur him. He was a man wi plenty a money. He done his land well, so he had good returns. His yard were alwiz full a stock—ivvery carner an it—and his barns were alwiz full a graian (grain). He done his feeulds well, fur his yard wuz alwiz full a dung. He trusted me wi the kays a the grinnery, and I was risponsible fur ivverything as was stooard thaiur.

"Well, a married son lived wi him, and a relation a the son's wife come to live wi em. He was a butcher by traiad, but ant got an very well; but he used to kill a ship occasionally and goo round the district and sell the mait: sometimes he used to goo to Teeam markut. I used to put the kays a the grinnery in a sartin pleeace. When I was in the cowhus, I sometimes see him a-meddlin about wi the kays and sometimes a-comin out a the grinnery with summut in a bag. When I went to look at what was happenin, I could see hooals in the heeaps a graian— and big hooals, too—so I maiad up mi mind to cleeur miself, fur if e dint, e should git miself shet up in Aiuhlsburry fur no fault a mi own, and very likely git transported. The moour I thought an it the gretter the deeanger I could see e was in. When it was found out, as it soon would a bin, as ivvery bushul as went in had bin booked, they ood a took no noatice a what I had to say, and if I had

then tried to put it an the right person they ood a said,
'Why dint you tell us an it befuur?' I felt I was in
danger a losing mi good naiam and being thought a thaif
as long as ivver e lived. So I maiad up mi mind to tell
ivverything. I went home and told mi wife what e was
a-gooing to do, and she agreed wi me.

"Fur the next few days I coont see mi mahster, as he
was ill; but when he come downsteears and got about,
and I run agen him the fust time, I said, 'Master, I be
gooin to tell ye summat's happenin with the carn in the
grinnery': so I toald him all. When I had done, I said,
'Now I know I shall a to goo fur it. Mrs. —— ull be
shuur to git me the sack.' 'No,' says he, 'I ull see to
that.' Howivver, it waunt long artur when I was a-milkin
in the cowhus, when she comes in and says, 'Will-yum,
come and do the churmin!' I said, 'I ull as soon as
I a maiad the cows all saiaf.' She says, 'You wunt do
as ye are toald'; so I said, 'I ull come as soon as ivver
I can, but I must tie the cows up saiafly.' I done this as
soon as ivver e could, and then went and done the churmin;
then I went back to the cowhus and finished mi milkin.
'Ah!' I thought, 'she a got me now.'

"Soon artur mi mahster come hooam, and in a little
while he walked acrass to me and said, 'Will-yum, I heeur
as ye woont do as ye were toald.' I says, 'Master, I coont
leeav the cows till I had maiad all saiaf.' He says, 'Heeur's
yur waik's money and goo at once.' 'No, master,' says I,
'I shant; you ull a to gi me another waik's pay in lieu a
noatice.' He says, 'I shant; you ant done as you were
toald, so you ull a to goo at once.' 'Then,' says I, 'I shant
leeav the pleeace until I git the two waiks' pay,' and
he had to gi it me; so I got the two waiks' waiages
and left.

"When I got hooam and toald mi wife, she says, 'You
ull git wurk somewheeur else. Dooant wurry. Summut
ull be shuur to come along,' and it did soon arter. Well,
I nivver bore em any malice, fur that would a bin a wrong
thing to do, and it waunt very long afuur a relation a
theirn axed me to wurk fur him, but I dint goo, as I had
got a very good pleeace in the farm not very fur away.

Howivver, I used to help em in my speear time, ispecially when they wer busy.

"One aivening a beautiful horse a theirn fell back wi the strangles, so they fot me and I did what e could, and at last got the horse round.   Mi old mahster, when he see the horse was better, said to me, 'Will-yum, you shull a a good suppur to-night, and a pint a beeur and as many moour as ye can drink.'   When the wurk was done I went in his kitchen wi him, and he went through into tuther rooms and toald em what to do.   I sot down in a cheear and waiated fur the suppur, and thaiur I sot till I almost went to slaip.   Nauthing come in.

"Arter a time he comes in and says, 'Will-yum, I hope you a injoyed yur suppur!'   'Thenkee,' says I, 'I ant had naiur a bit a nauthing to ett, and naiur a drap a beeur to drink.'   'You ant!' says he.   'No,' says I, 'I ant.' 'Well,' says he, 'I ull goo and see to that.'   He went in tuther room, and I heeurd him say to the son's wife who had got me the bag, 'How's this?   I toald you to gi Will-yum a good suppur, and as much beeur as he could drink, and you ant done it.   You ee-ant mahster in this house yit, and you wunt be while I be alive.   Goo and git him summut to ett and some beeur to drink at once.'

"Soon arter she brought a nice bit a baif in and some beeur and throwed it down at me as if she had bin a-faiding the pigs;   but I dint mind that.   I set to and had a good suppur wi plenty a beeur, and when I had had enoh I went hooam to bed.

"I knowed he was alwiz sorry fur gitting rid a me, and I alwiz felt I could a gone back whenivver I liked, but I dint goo.   He was a good farmer, and if ivvery farmer done his land as he done his, it ood be a good thing fur ivverybody.   I had no regrets, fur I alwiz sarved him faithfully.   Many a time did I goo back an dark winter nights artur supper to see if all was well in the staiables and cowhus, fur sometimes a cow or a horse gits loose and then damage is done.

"Ye can't realise what harm is done when the cattul beeant tied up saiafly—ony them as a sin it know what happuns.   Sometimes one ull slip its cheean an then goo a-wanderin about among tuthers all night, an then thaiur's shuur to be trouble afu-ur the marnin; an ye neeurly alwiz find the master-cow is the one as gits loose, an that's the one as is shu-ur to do moast damage."

(*His daughter leaves the room.*)

"That's mi dahter. She was in sarvice in London when mi poo-ur wife died. She was in a good pleeace, but she left it an come hooam to look artur me. If she ant a done I dunno what e should a done; I be affeard e should a to a gone to the Dumplin House. Howivver, she come an looked arter me ivver since, an I deearsay she ull to the eend.

"Well, I a now ain three yeeurs dooin nauthin. I had the rheumatics come an me an e was obliged to give up—an heeur e be, can't do much, ony do mi gardun an a few odd jobs about th' ouse; an yit e could do a good day's wurk if they ood ony leeav me. I feeul as healthy as e did yeeurs agoo, an can injoy mi meeuls as much as ivver e did, but e can't git about, e be so crippuld. I be ai-ahty-seven now, an a outlived ivverybody older than miself as e knowed when e was a boey: I feeul thankful that e a bin presarved an bin in good health all mi life. Sometimes when I be a-sittin heeur alooan, I think uv the ole feeaces as a gone, and then the blessins I a recaived through mi long life crap up in mi mind. The time seems pritty long some days, but I do a littul reeading, an that teeaks the dullniss awf. Ivvery marnin I reead two a the Psalms, an I do the saiam ivvery night; an I awfen reead some pree-ars, an they cumfurt me, but I do miss not bein able to goo to church an a Sunday. I should so like to goo to the pleeace wheeur God's neeam is honoured, an wheeur His peepul assemble, but e can't, as tis too fur away, an e can't walk. Howivver, I hope e shull some day, as I be havin a littul cheear an wheeuls maiad at the blacksmith's, so as e can wheeul miself down thaiur bi turnin th' handuls as I sit in the sait. I a got some money seeavd bi me to pay for 't and e be a seeavin what e can. If e could git down to sarvice ivvery Sunday, thaiur ood be summut to look forrad to, an the time woont hang so heavy as it do sometimes."

VISITOR. "I hope it will soon be ready for you."

MR. PLASTOW. "I shull git it soon, but e can't seeav much a week, as e ony got the Old Ai-age Pension to live an."

VISITOR. "Well, I should like to see every farmer's man who has worked hard all his life have every comfort he wants when he gets on in life."

MR. PLASTOW. "An they desarve it, fur thaiur's no class a men moour desarvin than what they be. They be up arly in the marnin, an they wurk laiat at night, an when they a wurked hard all ther lives they ought not to a the wurkhus a-steearin em in the feeace when they git too old fur work. When ye a got good, honest, straiaht-forrud, hard-workin laiabourers, they should a some reward. Nobody can tell the value uv a good laiabourer, whether he's a cattulman, shephurd, ur laiabourer. Ivvery one an em knows exactly what to do, an when tis done, the mahster knows its well done. You can't tell the value uv a good farm laiabourer to his mahster, an yit nobody thinks nauthin an him; he's the wust paid uv all an yit what would the country do wiout him? When ye git good mahsters an good laiabourers, ivverything goos an well. Thaiur's alwiz plenty a stock an the farm, plenty a laiabour, an plenty a dress an the land; then ye git plentiful craps. Uv cu-urse if the saison's bad you git some spoilt, but teeakin it an the whool, thaiur's plenty, an that's what we want right through the country. I know ye git bad mahsters as well as bad laiabourers—mahsters who ant got the money to treeat the soil as it should be treeated, an think they ull git out what they ant put in."

(Conversation is interrupted and resumed.)

"Ah! I was a-speeakin about bad cultivaiation. You git some farmers who add feeuld to feeuld and farm to farm, an ony imploy an em all as many as could ony propurly cultivaiat one farm. Then ye see the land niglected and not half done. Thaiur ant the laiabour to cleean it, and very soon the feeulds git covered wi waids and rubbish. Ye must a plenty a cattul in yur yard to put back an the land what ye a took frum it. If ye faid the land it ull faid you. Ye a got to treeat it like ye treeat anythink else, and then ye ull git yur returns. If ye starve it yeeur by yeeur and let it git overrun wi waids and rubbish, then ye git very little increeas—not much moour than what ye a put in ; but dress it well and kaip it cleean, then ye git the increeas. When I had pigs in mi sty, I used to put the pig-dung round the roots a the bushes in mi gardun, and I had currunts as big as churries, and goosburries as big as warnuts, and its jest like this in the ceeas a ivverything as grows an the land—it must a food to do its wurk.

"Some people think they can git summut out a nauthing—but they can't, and nivver wull. All mi life I a noaticed that land wi no dress gis very poour craps— short straa, little eeurs, and little kurnuls ; but land well dressed always gis good craps—long straa, long eeurs, and big kurnuls ; and I nivver yit sin big eeurs wi fat kurnuls an thin short straa, and nobody else nivver did. When carn is sold by weight, ant it better to taiak a peck out a the sack, than put a peck in ? That's the difference atween good and bad farmin. You must a cleean land, plenty a dress, and plenty a laiabour to git th' increeas, and when ye a got these, the increeas comes. And what cleeans the land like a good ploughsheear ! How it turns the ground ovur and distroys all the rubbish, ispecially when ye a got a good man behind the plough. I a bin a-reeadin out a the 'Ole Book' jest afuur you come in, and it says the 'time ull come when all the su-urds and speears shull be turned into ploughsheears and pruning hooks.' Then all the docks and the curlook and the cockuls and the thissuls and the nettuls and ivvery other kind a rubbish ull be distroyed. Then THE LAND ULL BE CLEEAN, and not only that, all malice and haiatred and covetousness ull be driven frum men's hearts. That ull be a happy time fur ivverybody, and it ull be shu-ur to come—the 'Ole Book' says so—but I shant live to see it. Ah ! that wull be a blessed time ! Thaiur ull be good mahsters ivverywheeur wi plenty a laiabour an the farm. The laiabourers ull git good waiages while the mahster gits the increeas. His yard ull be full a stock—ivvery carner an it—and his grinneries full a graian. His feeulds,

ivvery one an em, ull be well dressed, fur he's got plenty
a dung ; then thaiur ull be plenty fur ivverybody, fur the
increeas is shu-ur to follur.

"Wurkin an the land is lovely wurk—and in mi time
I wurked fu-urteen and fifteen hours a day, but that was
afuur the machines come about. We sowed by hand,
ripped by hand, and threshed wi the thraiul. It was
lovely wurk, and that was how it was done when I was a
young man. We used to dibble the sayd in, and I a dibbled
many a ai-acre a wheeat, beeans, wuts, and barley. Sometimes we used to sow broadcast. At harvist we cut wi a
sickle. We took a handful a carn and cut it, leeavin about
a foot a halm standin, so then the sheeavs waunt very big
and easily dried. When the sheeavs were stored in the
barn, it was most carn and a lot could be put in. Arter-
wards we cut the standin halm and mixed it wi the
cowdung, as that was the toughest, the tuther holdin the
corn was gin to the cattle as food.

"When threshin-time come we used to thresh wi a
thraiul, and this was the very best way too. The chaff is
swaiter, and the kurnuls a corn are not so much damaged
as when they goo through the brushes of a threshin
machine. Thaiur waunt a speck a dust an the threshin-
fluur when we used the thrail, and many a time we threshed
clover an it. Ivverything was swait and nice—different
to what tis at the present day. Ah ! tis lovely wurk, and
if I had mi tome ovur agen, I ud goo an the land. Some
peepul be shet up all day in offices and factories and nivver
have any fresh air—and this ant no good to em ; but
when ye wurk an the land ye are in the fresh air all the
time. Ye see the land ploughed an harrud, the sayd put
in, and then ther growth. At harvist time ye see all
round ye the results a yer laiabour. It is lovely wurk,
and if I had mi time ovur agen, and I was a boey a ten
yeeurs a age, I ud goo streeaht to a farm and git imployed.
Yis, I ood.

> I ood plough and sow,
>   (*after a pause*)
> And raip and mow,
> And be a farmer's boy."

L

THE MOST ENGLISH CORNER
OF ALL ENGLAND

By J. Wentworth Day

IF the rest of England were to sink suddenly and Norfolk
be left alone in the cold waters of the North Sea, it would
not, I think, bother itself unduly. For Norfolk is the
most individual county in all England. It is almost self-
contained, magnificently proud, and owes little to outside
sources of supply. It is ancient and historic, yet up-to-date
and energetic in the true essentials of good and simple
living. It is, in fact, England in little. Or perhaps
I should say Old England in little. That is true of East
Anglia as a whole.

Norfolk is the head and brains of East Anglia. And if
you ask me what is East Anglia, I shall reply that it is the

land of the Eastern Angles—the counties of Norfolk and Suffolk, with a bit of Essex and a slice of Cambridgeshire thrown in.

In the days when Boadicea was a puissant queen, half my own county of Cambridgeshire was a steaming sea of feverish bogs and shining mere, mile beyond mile of sighing reed-beds, green in Spring and tawny gold in Autumn. Mile on mile of waterways opened into the wildfowl-clouded meres of Whittlesey and Ramsey, Soham and Stretham, Uggmere and Holme, with a hundred others lesser known. Out of this fen stood the islands of Ely and Crowland, crowned by their mighty abbeys, and the lesser isles of Stonea, Manea, Stuntney, Henney, and a dozen others, with my own blunt-nosed peninsular of Wicken nosing broad-backed into the savage fens where the Cam, ungoverned and unbanked, carried sailing ships and trading barges to the city and port of Reach, mighty with its seven churches at the foot of that great ancient British earthwork, the Devil's Dyke, which still straddles the Newmarket uplands between the fens and the once wild woodlands of Wood Ditton, the Wood Ditched Town.

Those steamy swamps and mere which made the old savage fens, covered more than a quarter of a million acres of England. They stretched for more than sixty miles from north to south and thirty miles from east to west, those drowned lands and quaking reed-beds which swallowed great slices of Lincolnshire, Cambridgeshire, Huntingdon, Northamptonshire, and even south into Bedfordshire.

To the west they cut off East Anglia from the rest of England with an impassable sea. And to the south the great forests of Essex, of which Epping and Hainault with the tiny remnants of Takeley and Hatfield are the last echoes, cut off the rest of East Anglia from the south. So you may say that we in East Anglia were on an island, isolated from the rest of England by swamps, mere and savage forests, the haunts of wild men and wild boars, of stags and wolves, bitterns and fen eagles.

To-day the fens are drained and the forests are felled. Yet the ancient spirit of East Anglia endures strong and

unbroken. The individualism is still there. The country
that bred Hereward the Wake, the last of the Englishmen
to hold out against the Normans, bred also Nelson, the
man who broke Napoleon. It felt the fury of the Danes,
and their strong blood is in the East Anglian stock to-day.
You will meet their blue eyes and fair hair in villages
and on fishing smacks, just as on the Norfolk heaths and
in the flat villages of the black fens you will see the Jutish
type, high cheek-bones, narrow heads, black hair and
quick eyes, a type almost as restless and suspicious as
the Welsh.

Let us, therefore, consider Norfolk, the stronger partner
in this marriage of the North Folk and the South Folk
which made the counties of Norfolk and Suffolk.

They have most of the good things of life in Norfolk.
The biggest farms in England grow wheat for their bread
and barley for their beer; turnips for their sheep and
flax for your linen; mustard splashes its yellow hands
over thousands of acres of fir-bordered fields and rye
yellows palely on swelling uplands that look to the salt
marshes which border the North Sea.

There are no great manufacturing towns to stale the
air with banners of smoke or sour the spirits of those
who are tied for life to the wheels of industry. True, in
Norwich they make most things from aeroplanes to
ploughshares and mustard, and near Cambridge they
make jam by the ton. But those are industries almost
entirely of the soil, and in no case have they devoured
the countryside.

For I think of Norwich as a city of medieval streets
and Tudor doorways, dominated on the one hand by the
great Norman keep of its castle, and on the other by
the soaring beauty of that cathedral which Borrow con-
templated on Spring mornings and Crome painted in a
style and manner which was the genesis of one of the best
of all schools of English painting.

It is a different beauty from the classic charm and almost
unreal grace of Cambridge, where Italianate lightness has
been married with Tudor brickwork and half-timbered
buildings that were old when Henry the Sixth was on the

throne. And if you go north to King's Lynn you will find a different style of architecture altogether, the crow-stepped gables and Flemish spandrels of Bruge and Ghent—a style repeated with less distinction but equal Continental emphasis in Yarmouth, where strings of trawlers lie moored at the greatest fish quays in England, or steam fussily into the manifold perils of the North Sea. They catch more herring there than at any other town in the world.

If you want a different sort of beauty, you will find it in the magnificent churches in Suffolk, " silly Suffolk," because Selig was the old Saxon word for holy, and here in East Anglia men were devout in the dimmest days of early history. They reared great churches which stand like cathedrals on the plain, and built great abbeys which brought pilgrims from all England. The Shrine of Our Lady of Walsingham was a bourne for men of God from every country in the world. The Pedders Way, that ancient grass-grown track which winds like a ghost through deep woods and over windy heaths, knows the pale spirits of those kings and princes, merchants and pedlars, pilgrims and monks, who came on foot and on horse when Walsingham was a rival to Canterbury.

But if you go south into Suffolk over that wet watershed where the Waveney and the Little Ouse rise within a hundred yards of each other, one flowing east and one flowing west—if you dug a canal between the two you would make Norfolk an island in fact—you come to the villages of Lavenham and Kersey, which are to-day as perfect Tudor villages as any in England. There streets and houses stand and look precisely as they did when Elizabeth was on the throne and Sir Henry Hobart was building in Norfolk that great mansion of Blickling, which is as lovely in its way as any Montacute or Hampton Court.

I could tell of other villages and forgotten towns, of moated halls such as Oxburgh with its tattered banners and panelled walls, of grey castles and jackdaw-haunted priory ruins. But that would be merely a guide-book list. The richness is too great to be told baldly in a mere string of names.

The natural beauty is no less in diversity. Behind Sandringham, where the Kings of England have chosen to make their private home, there are heathery hills and tall woods standing like tapestries above valleys of shining water. Between Brandon and Thetford are wide, windy, miles of rusty heaths and ragged pines, the loneliest lands in all England, lands untouched since the Stone Age. The great bustard, the largest land bird in England, lingered on there after he had died out in every other county in England. Those heaths, as wild as any Scots moor, were the one place in England where King Edward the Seventh tried to introduce the red grouse. That was way back in memory, and they lingered on, with a few blackgame, for a quarter of a century afterwards. From those heaths and the barley uplands of North Norfolk, wide and windy as the downs of Southern England, you can go to the mighty sandhills of Holkham, that 43,000-acre estate of the Earl of Leicester which is a little feudal principality on its own, and find there great scarps of wind-tossed sand eighty and one hundred feet high. The sea-holly grows on their shifting slopes, and from their windy crests a man may look out over the shining floor of the sea with nothing between him and the savage morasses of Spitsbergen and the Lofoten Islands, where the wild geese breed and the great snowy owl hunts like a spectre on noiseless wings.

And, a little south by east of that manless sea-verge, there are the Broads, 5,000 acres of marshy lakes and wide waters, with two hundred miles of navigable waterways and many thousand more acres of green marshes and shining river valleys that have given colour and life to English painters from Constable to Arnesby Brown. The Broadsmen are a race apart, men semi-amphibious, living by fishing and fowling, by inland sailing and river trading, just as their great grandfathers lived before them. It is a country of wide landscapes and magnificent sunsets, of high skies and awesome dawns, a land with a dignity and beauty peculiarly its own, of silences that are more potent than words.

There is, in the heart of the Broads, the gaunt, bleakly

magnificent ruins of an abbey, St. Benet's-at-Holme, which, like Ely, was the last of the abbeys to defy the Norman invaders. But the story of St. Benet's, and its treacherous betrayal by a monk whom the Normans later hanged in the mocking magnificence of the abbot's vestments for which he had bargained at his price, is little known. No Charles Kingsley has yet arisen to tell the story of that unsung defiance of the abbot and his monks holding out for the last of England in the misty marshes of nine hundred years ago.

So you see that this land of East Anglia has all sorts of diversities of land and water, of old houses and great churches, of untrodden heaths and silent waterways, to give us still a lingering picture of what was once the face of that older England which the Dane knew and the Norman conquered, which the Saxon loved with his last fighting breath and which, as yet, is unspoilt and untamed by hedgerows and hard roads, not yet stifled by factory chimneys or soiled by the red raw sores of that bungalow development which has spoiled the face and prostituted the soul of what was once the loveliest country.

I said that there are great farmers in Norfolk. So, too, are there great landowners of the old, fine type, whose paternal benevolence, good guidance, and unselfish leadership helped to form the spirit of England. There are landowners like Lord Hastings, whose family has been seated on its own lands at Melton Constable for close on a thousand years; names like L'Estrange which you will find in Doomsday Book and De Greys who have been at Merton Hall for six centuries, and Hamonds who were there in Saxon days, and Bedingfields whose moated hall is a page of splendid, muted history.

It was Townshend of Raynham who wrought one of the greatest revolutions in agriculture when he taught farmers to grow turnips and introduced the four-course system. It was " Coke of Norfolk," ancestor of the presant Lord Leicester, who made sheep, wheat and barley grow on an estate which was formerly a wilderness, until to-day Holkham stands to all the world as a model of good farming and benevolent land ownership. One of the

Cokes gave us, in his "Laws of England," a very proper and foundation stone of our judicial system. And if you went to Holkham to-day, as I did last year, you would find that the farmers and tenants on that great estate speak to-day of the present Lord Leicester even as William Cobbett found that they spoke of his forebear a hundred years ago, when he said in his diary, "everyone speaks of the Earl of Leicester as children would speak, in endearing terms, of a fond parent."

With the big landowners there are equally big farmers. Consider, for instance, Mr. Billy Parker who, with his sons, farms 40,000 acres. He is the greatest farmer in all England. There is Major Birkbeck at West Acre, High House, who owns and farms around about 10,000 acres, and the Masons who farm nearly 20,000 acres, and Mr. Henry Thompson of Middleton who farms another 10,000 acres, and then there are Keiths and Ringers and others who think and farm in tens of thousands of acres. They do things on a big scale in this bold land that is unique and apart from the rest of England.

You can hunt the fox, the stag, the hare, or the otter with packs of hounds of the four different sorts ; you can catch sea trout up to six and seven pounds in weight in little rivers whose names I would not quote for a ransom, and you can shoot pheasants and partridges, wild geese, duck and snipe in a manner and on a scale unequalled elsewhere in England and without peer in the world.

Norfolk shooting has always been world-famous, not only for the mere size of the bags, but because of the high quality of the actual shooting and the peculiar natural quality of the Norfolk soil and atmosphere as a natural game country. To begin with, it is the driest county in England, with the lowest rainfall. This means that partridge chicks and young pheasants have a very high chance of survival in Spring and early Summer, the months when, in most counties, they are likeliest to perish during heavy rains.

The dry, porous quality of the soil is another natural asset, for rains quickly drain away and natural cover such as bracken, heather and broom flourish abundantly, too much so in some districts.

The result is that not only is it easy to rear game in large quantities, but there is always a big reservoir of hardy, wild-bred birds to fall back on and to impart quality and endurance to the reared stock.

Norfolk is particularly lucky, also, from the point of view of both the wildfowler and the naturalist since, from its geographical position, as a blunt shoulder of England jutting boldly into the North Sea, it is the natural landing ground for migrant birds from the north and the east. Wild geese, ducks, waders, snipe, woodcock, and a host of small birds, which annually journey from north to south, touch Norfolk on their first " hop." Many stay to breed. The result is that Norfolk has a longer and more interesting list of rare birds to its credit than any other county in England. Practically every bird on the British list, from the golden eagle and the much rarer white-tailed eagle to the flamingo, the stork, the glossy ibis, and the tiny fire-crested wren has been seen or shot in Norfolk. The Broads, with their winding rivers, immense tracts of marshland, and shining meres, are one of the several magnets which Norfolk holds out to the wing-weary traveller from Scandinavia, Spitsbergen, the Finnish lakes or the Russian forests.

Hickling Broad which, with Whiteslea and Heigham Sounds, covers six hundred acres of water, with vast surrounding reed-beds and half-drained marshes, is the most interesting marshland bird sanctuary in England. It is the property of Lord Desborough, who has there preserved a unique home for wildfowl and rare marsh birds. Several pairs of bitterns breed every year, and the Montagu's harrier and the short-eared owl also nest regularly, while the rarer marsh harrier and the hen harrier are seen practically every year. The bearded tit or " reed pheasant," which was almost extinct in England a few years ago, has now firmly established itself at Hickling, safe from egg collectors and those who consider that a rare bird looks better stuffed in a glass case than alive and beautiful in its natural surroundings. This tiny delicately marked little bird, with its graceful long tail and dark moustaches, creeps like a mouse through the tall reeds, swinging head downwards and ringing its clear, bell-like note.

I have been on Hickling in a gun-punt on a Winter's day, and seen the rare and wonderful sight of nearly two thousand wildfowl on the wing at once—teams of mallard, wigeon, tufted duck and teal, with pintail, smew and pochards among them. Coot were on the water and in the air in hundreds. In fact, we shot six hundred that day, for it was one of the great annual coot-drives, when every sportsman and marshman for miles around turns out with a boat and a gun to thin down the myriads of these black fowl which each Winter descend upon the Broad in thousands and tear up the water weeds voraciously.

That day we saw wild geese, wild swans, several harriers and a bittern, and I met a man who, earlier in the year, had seen an avocet stepping delicately, a slender vision in black and white, in the shallow waters of a marsh pool. There have been years when more than a thousand coots have been shot in one day on Hickling and distributed among the marshmen and cottage housewives, to whom coot pie is a great delicacy. Skinned, part-boiled in milk, and then baked in a pie, they are as delicate as a spring chicken.

During the nesting season the Hickling waters and marshes are strictly preserved. Rare birds and common water fowl are given every encouragement to breed. Miss E. L. Turner has told the story of Hickling and its bird life in her charming book, "Broadland Birds." Those who want to know more about sport in Broadland should pick up the late Nicholas Everitt's charming and compendious work, "Broadland Sport," whilst to complete the library, W. A. Dutt's beautiful work, "The Norfolk Broads," makes the indivisible trinity. The reproductions in colour of the pictures of that great bird artist, the late Frank Southgate, are alone worth the price of the latter book, whilst those who want first-class modern pictures of Broadland birds and life, should go to Messrs. Vicars' Galleries, or Messrs. Ackerman's Picture Shop in

Old Bond Street and see, or buy, the original water-colours of J. C. Harrison, Roland Green and Peter Scott. Roland Green, a shy and delightful man, lives in an old windmill at the Hickling end of the Broad.

He has decorated Lord Desborough's reed-thatched bungalow, which stands on a little green plot of flowers and grass by the Broadside, with the most delightful friezes of local bird life. They show the life of the Broads from Spring to Winter, terns dipping, bitterns nesting, ducks asleep in Spring sunlight, harriers beating the marshes like setters, and reed pheasants swinging on bending reeds like mice. It is a unique gallery of the work of a modest and unassuming artist whose art deserves wider recognition.

A mile or two away Major Anthony Buxton has another private bird sanctuary covering sixteen hundred acres of marshes, water, woods and cornfields, with a range of wild sand-hills by the sea. That is the Horsey Hall Estate, which includes Horsey Mere of about two hundred and thirty acres of water, lying between the sand-hills and the sea, and the Broads. A hundred years ago sea-eagles, now practically extinct, were so common at Horsey that Lubbock records having seen five or six in the air at once.

Both Major Buxton and Lord Desborough are good landowners and sensible sportsmen, who have proved beyond a shadow of doubt that a reasonable amount of shooting and the preservation of rare and beautiful birds can easily go hand in hand.

And if I were to advise you to look for another wild place, since wild places are the true background to all essential human knowledge and beauty, I should say go to Scolt Head. Scolt Head is that island of sand dunes, saltings and mud-flats which lies off the north coast of Norfolk to seaward of the village of Burnham Overy. Scolt Head is one of the few places still left in this England which have never known the brick foundation of a house, the thrust of a ploughshare or the grind of wheels. It is, and always has been, a half-land, a sort of no-man's land, set like an unconsidered jewel between the windy solitudes of the North Sea and the flat, purple miles of sea lavender, laced by shining creeks, which lie to the landward. There are sand dunes on Scolt Head so sharp in their scarps that they have all the sense and might of little mountains. They cut sharp silhouettes against the deep china blue of July skies, and catch in their tawny crests the unhindered blast of Winter winds from the Arctic. They have the contours in miniature, and the chills in reality, of mountains.

Because Scolt Head juts into the northern sea in such uncompromising loneliness it has, in microcosm, the best and the rarest, the wariest and the shyest of all the long and glittering list of rare migrants to its credit. To read a tithe of the names of its rare birds would be to take an historic chapter from the pages of British ornithology.

It was a few years after the end of the last war that the late Lord Leicester, that good and wise landowner, sold Scolt Head for a mere tittle of money, £500 to wit, to the Norfolk and Norwich Naturalists' Trust. Doctor Sidney Long, who did a momentous work for Norfolk natural history as honorary secretary to that Trust, took it on him to see that Scolt Head was preserved as a national resting place and reservoir of rare birds. A watcher was appointed, a wooden hut was set up, and Scolt Head became a true sanctuary.

Perhaps, for a time, a little too much was written about it. Too many people went to watch the terns nesting, and too many would-be naturalists marched about like inquisitive telegraph poles, with glasses glued to their eyes and avid notebooks in their pockets. The same thing happened at Blakeney Point. It is inevitable when you create what is virtually a public sanctuary. It no longer remains private for the birds. That is one thing which the National Trust will have to consider in a longer sense now that it has opened its increasingly bureaucratic maw to swallow up beauty spots of England which, for centuries, have been preserved by judicious and responsible landowners. The moment a possession becomes completely public property it is invariably tarnished. Indiscipline, untidiness and tramplings down follow in the train of unbridled freedom.

However, the trippers and the peering photographers with their museum minds and long-focus lenses disappear as soon as the north-east wind whistles down from the Arctic. The first snowflakes send them scuttling for buns and the fireside. Then it is, when the long rollers come in on the beach with a wintry hiss, when the sand hardens in the grip of the frost and the first thin fingers of ice shoot out overnight across the surface of broad and marsh pool, that the hosts of waders, the black battalions of duck, and the chanting cohorts of geese come down from the bitterness of Baltic beaches and the whitening wildernesses of Finnish fens, from the cold solitudes of Scandinavian fells and the ancient gloom of lichened woods. You might see almost anything then on these dunes or treading in the clear half-light of dawn in the shallow pools—anything from a woodcock crouching sleepy-eyed under the leeward side of a tussock, to a peregrine beating on scimitar wings up the lonely miles of houseless coasts. There will be snow buntings coming in like snowflakes, lonely and forlorn; brent geese, which last knew the elfin wastes of Novaya Zembla; and, perhaps once in a generation, a great snowy owl, large almost as an eagle, terrifying with his tiger eyes, dropping in on heavy wings like a Nordic spectre from the land of Thor.

To see the full tale of this long and noble roll of Norfolk birds, a glittering page in British ornithology, go to the Castle Museum at Norwich where, in that great Norman Keep, once a prison, they reach from floor to ceiling, tier upon tier of wanderers. Major Birkbeck has probably the finest private collection in all Norfolk at West Acre High House, in the great hall, but that is no incitement for the inquisitive stranger to write and invade his house.

There is, or was if German bombs have not destroyed it, an equally notable collection in the Tollhouse at Yarmouth, and many a private collection, each with its feathered notables, in a score of country houses throughout the county. Perhaps the finest group of the now extinct bustard was at Congham House, Mr. Robert Elwes's place near Hillington, but they, alas, cock bird, hen bird, young and eggs, were destroyed by fire some years ago. I had in my own small collection one of the last Norfolk bustards killed ninety years ago on the borders of Croxton, Elveden and Merton, but that, too, vanished at the beginning of the war.   I still have a Cambridgeshire bird, believed to be the last one killed in the county in 1842, but it is a hen, and not comparable with the magnificent cock bird from Merton whose shadow I mourn.

North Norfolk owes, as indeed does all England, an immense debt to its great landowners, who have beautified its face, preserved its coastline, and encouraged its rare birds, from the L'Estranges who were at Huntstanton Hall in medieval days, to the King at Sandringham, Lord Leicester at Holkam, Lord Suffield at Gunton, and a score of smaller properties between.   They have saved this corner of England which the speculative builder, the tripper-exploiter and the sprawling holiday camp might so easily have ruined and reduced to untidy " bungalowsis " and marine slumdom, as they have done on so many other miles of coastland.

It is extraordinary how wild birds will come back, by instinct and choice, to their ancient haunts if once they are given encouragement, peace and natural food. I proved this to a remarkable degree when, in 1935, I bought a few hundred acres of half-drained, reedy and lonely fenland near Burwell in Cambridgeshire.   It was useless as farm-land, under water half the year, dangerous for cattle and horses which got bogged in its peaty softnesses, and utterly roadless and houseless.   It lay between Burwell and Reach Lodes—a windy, flat, wild triangle of reed-beds and stinking pools, creamy with meadow-sweet in Summer, shining with Autumn floods in the tail of the year.   The clear destiny for such a place was to let the floods have their way and the land revert to wild fens.   The Winter gales came and blew down the black-boarded draining mill.   The floods stayed.   The waters spread until a hundred and eighty acres became one great, shining, straggling broad, walled by tall reeds, islanded by clumps of savage-edged sedges and dotted here and there by wind-bent willows.

Within a year the bitterns, which had not been seen for half a century, returned to nest.   Marsh harriers and Montagu harriers came back to breed and hawk.   The hen harrier beat the Autumn levels.   Duck of all sorts poured in from the windy fen skies—mallard and teal, pochard and shoveller, tufted duck, and even the rare and delicate little garganey teal.   Gadwall reared their young and once, on a fantastic September morn when the white mists lifted like rent blankets from the face of the waters, I saw six Egyptian cattle egrets—unbelievable visitors, probably from Whipsnade or Lilford.   Wild geese came in Winter, both grey and bean, and wild swans filled the Winter sky with the windy harp-notes of their wings. Herons, grey and immaculate, fished the shallow pools, and peewits fell on stumbling wings and wept their mournful laments.   There were redshank like dancers in the peaty, brown shallows, and reed warblers creeping like mice among the reeds.   The grasshopper warbler bewitched the Summer night with his reeling songs, and terns in Summer screamed thinly in the bright air or fell like flashing plummets into the waters where pike swirled and roach and rudd moved in slow, golden shoals.

For seven years it was a place of beauty and solitude, a lost recaptured echo of the old, wild fens of Stuart England.   In Summer it was starred with water lilies, pale yellow with meadow-sweet, a network of glittering waterways and tall green reeds which would hide a man in a punt for a day and leave him to an utter solitude of time and space.   In Autumn the great reed-beds turned rusty gold, then tawny, till they faded into the burnt brown of Winter, and the waters took on the steel of January skies.

It was too good to last, that place of beauty and of birds. The war came and the drainers came.   Tunnels were dug, and slowly the waters fell.   The reeds stood dry and rustling in forlorn, waterless desolation.   They were mown down and burnt in swirling clouds of thick smoke which rolled across the country for miles, until even distant Newmarket was blanketed one afternoon by the prairie fires which wiped out that last echo of an older and lovelier England. To-day the land is black, rich and unbeautiful.

Fortunately there are still broads, marshes, heaths, and long miles of sand-hills in Norfolk untouched even by the relentless materialism of war, although, to be sure, her ancient silences are now made hideous by the constant roar of aircraft. Aerodromes have sprung up like mush-rooms. Many a remote parish which, five years ago, was as peaceful as an eighteenth century village, has seen woodlands levelled, cornfields ruined and wild brecks disappear under tarmac in order that the outer bastions of England shall be safe. That cannot be helped. But it will be profoundly interesting to see whether these immense strings of airfields are all kept in commission after the war. Some will return inevitably to cultivation, but if only a strategic line of them is maintained in commission down the East coast it will mean that the once silent skies of East Anglia will remain a Charing Cross of the air. Those of us who knew the grace and spacious peace of Norfolk before the war will be left with no more than a lovely memory.

You never know what is going to turn up in Norfolk. It is a county of exciting unexpectedness. For example, I once was shooting at Croxton Park, Sir William Gentle's place, standing silent and alone in a ride which led from the heat-haze of miles of bracken and heather into the dim resinous aisles of a big fir wood. Suddenly a red stag with a magnificent head, twelve atop, stepped out, a tawny ghost, from among the trees and stood watching me. Who would expect to see a wild red stag at large on the edge of a Norfolk heath in a fir wood full of cooing pigeons and skulking pheasants ? I would have sworn that there were no wild red deer at large nearer than Scotland.

" Oh, he's been here for years," said Sir William, as we lunched later, sitting on a log. " No one knows where he came from, but I'm certain he's not a park stag, and he has now quite made friends with us—comes up to the keeper's cottage gate to be fed every morning, but he'll never let you get near enough to touch him. I only wish I could find him a wife."

That red stag was quite as unexpected as the Indian barking deer which a keeper shot, to his utter astonishment, in some reed-beds near West Harling one sunny day fifteen years ago. No one ever found out where that strange visitor came from.

But when a woman encountered a bear shambling along in the gloaming by the side of the lonely heath road which runs up by Bagmoor on the Merton property, there was an explanation. He had given his circus the slip and gone for a stroll.

I received a letter as I was writing this chapter from a friend, Mrs. Jamieson, who lives in that lovely old house called The Canons at Thetford, the city of ghosts and vanished kings. The mighty Hugh Bigod, one-time lord of half East Anglia, the man whose armies defied the King, lies buried under the lawn hard by the end of the ruined chapel of the Praemonstratensian Friars, the chapel where on a bright May morning Doctor Jamieson and his wife heard the ghostly chanting of an unseen choir and the footsteps and solemn intonings of a spectral monk reading a lesson in Latin.

In this letter Mrs. Jamieson said, "We have just unearthed a stone coffin which we are almost certain contains the remains of Swayne, the father of Canute. You must come for the reinterment on 6th July." Alas, I was unable to go to that reburial of the dusty bones of a Saxon King who died near enough a thousand years ago. But it was not in the least surprising that such a king was to be dug up in a Norfolk garden or that such a cool, unflustered announcement of so momentous a discovery should come from a Norfolk friend.

They learn to expect anything in that county where the people of at least one village still talk the language of Neolithic man. That is at Weeting on the Suffolk border, hard by Brandon. There they have the last flint pits in England, where flints are dug from the bowels of the earth and knapped in shapes fit for gun flints, tinder lighters, skinning knives, and the rest, by village craftsmen, whose strange skill and stranger trade-terms have come down unbroken since the dim days of the Stone Age. Some

M

of the stag-horn picks used by those skin-clad miners
in the dusty dawn of the world were found only a few
years ago in one of the galleries leading off the main
flint pit.   They had been there sticking in the earth wall
before Christ walked in Galilee.   They call these pits
Grimes's graves, for the simple reason that in East Anglia
we still believe in witches and the devil, and the devil is
still Grimma, his old Saxon name.

In my own fen at home, at Wicken in Cambridgeshire,
we found a skull of Bos Urus, the great wild ox, mighty
as a bison, lying blackened in the peat, with a flint axe
still sticking in its forehead where the Stone Age hunter
had driven it with all the force of his Simian arm.   And
not far off, in Burwell Fen, where I had that lovely sanctuary
of birds and wild flowers and lily-starred waters which is
now potato land, they found the dead, dried and pickled
body of a fenman of a thousand years ago, standing bolt
upright in the remains of a dug-out canoe.   His long
black hair hung down the leather skin of his face and
neck.   His right hand was poised and crooked as though
to throw a spear, whilst on his legs were still the leather
buskins and cross garterings.   He could not survive the
outer air and crumbled too soon into desiccation and dust.

But when I think of Norfolk I think not only of these
antique surprises and macabre survivals but of high,
blue skies and drifting cloud masses coming in on the
sea winds from the Wash.   I think of hot September days,
shooting at Merton or Croxton or Lynford or on the
fens down at Marham, or other days, bitter Winter dawns
under the sand-hills at Wells, or with the wind whistling
like a rattle of musketry through the tall reeds by Cley
salt lagoons.   I think of lovely Tudor manor houses
and old moated halls like Elsing, of farmhouses, flint-built
and red-tiled, standing like forts in the heart of forgotten
heaths or crouching by the marsh-side with faces set
defiantly to the seas.

I think of long days riding on Robert, my old hunter,
from Euston, that lovely house which is half English
history, just on the Suffolk border to Thetford, and by
the heath roads to Brandon and then on to Methwold,

where the sandy upland falls suddenly to the black sea
of the fens, and the fens go marching away with their
straight dykes and files of willows, like green, slender
soldiery, away into the unguessed horizons of Lincolnshire.

And from Methwold we rode to Cockley Cley and to
Swaffham, that sleeping beauty of an eighteenth century
house, and from there up to Hillington and Sandringham
and away along the coast, by the vastness of the saltings
and the sea, under the whimper of curlews' wings, to
Wells with its maltings and quays and Blakeney with its
harbour and cobbled streets until, on Salthouse Heath a
tempest blew off the sea, the wind thundered in the pines,
the North Sea rose in bottle-green fury and lashed itself
white and then, in a God-sent moment, the sun came out,
the wind blew away with a whisk and a flourish, and all
the long Norfolk coast, its marshes and sea lavender, its
sand-hills and pine dunes, its crawling creeks and crisp
beaches, was green and blue and tawny and gold in the
clear light of a Norfolk morning.

It was a moment for Borrow, a flicker of time for a
Constable—a moment so much a part of the loveliness
and spirit of Norfolk that I, for my part, would wish no
other county in the world wherein to live and die.

TRIBUTE TO COMELY KENT
AND HER ANCIENT LIBERTIES

By KATHARINE PEARCE

" INVICTA "—men of Kent and Kentish men—oast houses,
hop gardens—cherry orchards—fresh picked Kentish
strawberries in Covent Garden—Romney Marsh sheep
in Australia and Patagonia—white cliffs of Dover—joy
of buttered toast and English tea as the boat train
dashes through the welcome green fields and neat
hedgerows of Kent when one has been out of England
for some time—Kentish oysters on the dinner tables of
ancient Rome—Julius Cæsar—early British and Roman
iron mines—railings from a Kentish iron foundry
round St. Paul's—Kent, " The Saxon Shore," and the
watch for the Anglo-Saxon pirates—Hengist and Horsa—
St. Augustine—the watch for the Danes—Canute and

Sandwich — Harold of Kent, the last Anglo - Saxon
" hallowed to be king "—the watch for the Normans—
William the Conqueror grants the continuation of their
ancient laws and customs to the men of Kent—Cinque
Ports and French pirates—the Black Prince and the Fair
Maid of Kent—Flemings and the wool trade—Chaucer
and the *Canterbury Tales* — Huguenot papermakers —
Shakespeare folios printed on Kentish paper—the watch
for the Spaniards — smugglers — the watch for the
Dutch—romances of the Dover and Folkestone packet
boats—the watch for Napoleon—Canterbury Cricket Week
and cricket on every village green—popularity of bell
ringing as an art and sport in Kent—" the guns that roared
in Flanders " in 1914-1918 heard in Kent—Dunkirk and
the Kentish boatmen—the Battle of Britain and its trails
in the Kentish sky—men of Kent and Kentish men in
the forefront of the battle in mediæval times, and again in
the forefront in North Africa in 1943—still " invicta "—
Kent, a sturdy and a truly comely county. Thus the
records in my brain tick over at the mention of Kent.

The first history of an English county to be published
was " The Perambulations of Kent," written by William
Lambarde in 1570, and in it he tells us that " the common
people, or yeomanrie (for so they be called of the Saxon
word *gemen* which signifieth common) is nowhere more
free and joily than in his shire." And free and jolly
the people of Kent remain to this day, and joyful in its
loveliness is the Kentish countryside as it looks in on
the south-eastern outskirts of London, or the wharfside
towns of the Thames Estuary, and as it goes pleasantly
on its flowery way, by Weald and Down, to show a fearless
smiling face to friend and foe along the Channel. A
landscape whose hills and valleys fold into one another
with smooth ancient curves. What a story lies behind
this earliest inhabited, earliest cultivated corner or cantium
of Britain !

" *Old Andred's Weald at length doth take his time to tell*
    The changes of the World that since his youth befell."

Changes there have been indeed since the Megalosaurus
galumped, and the Perodactyle hopped in Wealden day,

and the Ichthyosaurus disported himself in some sea which was the remote predecessor of the English Channel, leaving their bones to be discovered near Maidstone and Hythe, so that small boys of the nineteenth and twentieth centuries A.D. might delight in the reconstructed skeletons of these saurions at South Kensington Museum and in the gardens of the Crystal Palace.

Some great river flowing from the north-west, possibly out of the legendary continent of Atlantis, brought with it the clay deposit which formed the Weald; then the sea covered the delta which the river had built up, and when the land emerged once more it had greensand hills and ridges set upon the clay plateau, as well as the ocean-formed hills of chalk which lie to the north and east. Palms and crocodiles once flourished in what is now the Thames Valley, then came the Ice Age, and that in turn gave place to a milder climate, but while the ice still lingered in northern Britain, and the chalk hills of Kent and Picardy were one continuous range, across the valley which is now the Straits of Dover came the woolly rhinoceros, the hippopotamus, the straight-tusked elephant, the mammoth, the cave bear, the hyena, the elk, and the reindeer, with paleolithic man, " pursuing and pursued," and scattering over Kent his tools and weapons to be collected by his successors so many thousands of years later that one cannot compute the exact length of the intervening space of time.

To-day we take a somewhat dim and patronizing view of the struggles and hardships of life in caveman days, but if a local inhabitant of the paleolithic period had returned to Kent in 1940 during an air raid, he would not have been unduly impressed by the civilizing influence of all those thousands and thousands of years of progress ! On the contrary, he might well have sighed for the comfortable security of his cave, and longed for the less alarming attentions of a mammoth or a woolly rhinoceros, instead of those he had from a " cultured " modern German, who sprayed him with machine-gun bullets from a monster aeroplane.

After what we call the Paleolithic Age came the

Neolithic Age; whether or not the Straits of Dover existed in early Neolithic times is not known, but the land in the south of Britain certainly then stood much above its present level, and the channel, if any, must have been very narrow.   With Neolithic man came the ox, the dog, the sheep, the goat and the hog, and life in Kent began to be more like that of early historic times.   Traces of the Neolithic inhabitants have been found all over Kent, and at Grovehurst, near Sittingbourne, and Hayes Common, can be seen sites of their settlements, and the outlines of the sunk floors of the huts in which they lived, while the forerunner of our hedgerows may possibly be traced in " the thickset hedge, undoubtedly of pre-historic origin, that marks the line along which the Downs were bounded by the Wealden forest."

The Neolithic Age was followed by the Bronze Age, and although it is difficult to say at what date bronze was first introduced into Britain, it seems to have been in use here in 2000 B.C.   Archæological evidence shows that the men of Kent at this time were tillers of the soil and fellers of the forest, and had a multiplicity of tools and weapons.   These Bronze Age people were apparently rather " dressy," wore wool and linen, and decorated themselves with ornaments, necklaces, and buttons of ivory, jet, glass, gold, amber and bronze, and also used razors.

The Bronze Age merged into the Iron Age, and, during the Iron Age, Celtic tribes came to this island.   The Kentish labourer of to-day, who goes to his " pub " for a glass of beer after his work is done, has more than he probably realizes in common with his ancestors of over 2,000 years ago, for they too herded their flocks, tilled the soil, worked in mines, and drank their beer with gusto, when Kent was still but on the outermost fringe of the civilized world.   When Pythias, who was probably a contemporary of Alexander the Great (356-223 B.C.) did a tour round Britain, a race known as the Brythons were established here, and agriculture was prevalent throughout the country ; wheat and other cereals being grown in the south, but in the north oats only.   Pythias particularly noticed that corn was not thrashed in the open, but carried to barns, and that it was used for brewing beer as well as for food.

With the coming of Cæsar, the days of history begin, and Julius Caius, " the all-accomplished statesman, the splendid orator, the man of elegant habits and polished taste," landing in Kent in 55 B.C., recorded that " the number of the people is countless, and their buildings exceedingly numerous . . . there is timber of every description, except beech and fir . . . the most civilized of all these nations are they who inhabit Kent."

The Cantii whom Cæsar encountered were a Celtic tribe, the Belgae, and were certainly no naked savages. They wore " braccae," in other words breeches or trousers, made of striped or chequered cloth, tunics which reached to below the knee, cloaks which were usually blue or black in colour, and shoes of untanned leather. Their hair was long, and many favoured a blond tint achieved by the use of a bleaching soap (soap being a Celtic invention), and they shaved their beards but cultivated long moustaches. They also, rather regrettably, dyed themselves with woad when going into battle, and despite the compliments which Cæsar paid to their valour, their skill in horsemanship, and their comparative civilization, few people now remember anything about them except that they had a barbarous habit of painting themselves blue !

Kent was Celtic for about 700 years and under Roman rule for over 400 years, and although it subsequently became predominantly Anglo-Saxon (or rather Anglo-Jutish) it did not change its name or character. As early as A.D. 488 the new owners of the land were calling themselves " men of Kent," and, as a foreign historian has said, " even at a slight glance over the history of England we must be repeatedly reminded of the distinguishing nationality of the men of Kent."

My own experience of Kent is that to live there is to become history-minded, and that the yeomanry or common people are unusually conscious of the past, and of their own ancestry.

When I set up house in the Weald, the man who laid my carpets told me his family came from Lympne, and I found that he was speaking of Norman times when his family, one of the most ancient in all Kent, had been great land owners. I was also intrigued to discover that his name was identical with that of the Roman legion who had garrisoned the Lympne district. One of the builder's workmen knew that his family were Anglo-Saxons, and that his girl friend's family had been men of note in Tudor times. The vanman who brought my luggage had an unusual name, and told me that his people came from another part of Kent where they had owned land in mediæval times, and sure enough I found their name in fifteenth century records of that neighbourhood. The garage man said he was Flemish, and that his people came to Kent in Edward III's time. The girl from the village, who came to clean, said she was of French descent, and I was able to identify her family as being Huguenots.

The name of my house and the land on which it stood was of Anglo-Saxon origin, the name of a neighbouring house and hamlet was of Celtic origin, the nearest village and manor were mentioned in Domesday Book; a few miles away was an iron mine last worked in Roman days; not far off were the earthworks of a large early Iron Age settlement. We drove to the main line station along what has been a Roman highway; through the woods went another Roman road, the metal of which lay about plentifully; now disused sunken mediæval roads were everywhere, and some of the tracks across the woody hills may even have been among " the many well-known roads and paths through the forest " which Cæsar mentioned. Down in the marsh a large Danish army had encamped in A.D. 893, and the destruction they caused was still spoken of in neighbouring villages. In the same place Harold assembled his " miscellaneous rout of country people " before marching into Surrey to meet William.

A workman showed me a bronze implement, identified by the British Museum as being about 3,000 years old, which he had found near his cottage; many people had

unearthed Roman coins when ploughing ; the bones of a
whale were said to have been found on the top of a neighbouring hill ; my friends found sea shells while making
a new garden on another hill-top ; my cook had tales
of a richly decorated Saxon shield and ornaments which
were found in a grave in the garden of the last place in
which she worked ; in the State papers of Henry VIII's
reign, I read interesting letters written to Cardinal Wolsey
from what is now a farmhouse a few miles from our
village, but which was then an important manor.

All a jumble of facts from the long, long story of Kent,
but making the past very real.

There was no castle, or famous historic mansion, no
lordly Norman family to keep alive by its great possessions
the memories of other days, but the common people
were nearly all of families who were known to the county
throughout hundreds of years.   Celts, Romans, Angles,
Danes, Normans, Flemings, and French Huguenots had
probably contributed to their blood, but as Kent remained
Kent, so its people became, and remained, distinctively
Kentish, and are still the same sturdy folk of whom the
early chronicler, John of Salisbury, wrote, " They do to this
day claim the honour of the first ranks and the first charge in
all engagements."   Our villagers were not on the whole at
all familiar with history as it is set out in books, but many of
them talked to me of this traditional claim which had
evidently been old in Norman times.   They also quoted the
mediæval rhyme, " the father to the bough, the son to the
plough," and knew of the Kentish law of " gavelkind "
which, among other things, lays down that though the
father be hanged, the son is nevertheless entitled to his due
share of his father's property.   I am afraid I knew nothing
of " gavelkind " myself when I went to Kent. but I had
not been there more than a few weeks when I began
to hear of it.   William the Conqueror is said to have had
the same experience, for according to a very persistent
popular belief, the men of Kent waylaid him on his march
to London and successfully parleyed with him about
" gavelkind " and their other ancient laws and liberties.
Thomas Sprot, a Canterbury monk who lived in the

reign of Edward I, gave the story in his chronicles, and
Lambarde quotes Sprot (to whom he wrongly refers
as " Spot ") as his authority for the following version :—

> " ech man got him a greene bough in his hand and bare it over
> his head in such sort as when the Duke approached he was
> much amazed therewith, thinking at first that it had been
> some miraculous woode that moved towards him. But they,
> as soone as hee came within hearing, cast away their boughs
> from them, and, at the sounde of a trumpet, bewraied their
> weapons, and withall dispatched towards him a messenger,
> which spake unto him in this manner, ' The commons of
> Kent, most noble Duke, are readie to offer thee either peace
> or warre at thine owne choyce and election ; peace with
> their faithfull obedience if thou wilt permit them to enjoy
> their ancient liberties ; warre, and that most deadly, if thou
> denie it them.' Now when the Duke heard this, and con-
> sidered that the danger of deniall was great, and that the
> thing desired was but small, he forthwith, more wisely than
> willingly, yeelded to their request."

Camden (in his *Britania*, published 1637) says that the
ancient liberty which the men of Kent especially wished
to retain was the law " which they call Gavelkind, *Give
all Kinne*, by which they are not so bound by copyhold,
customarie tenures, or tennant-right, as in other parts of
England, but in manner every man is a freeholder and hath
some part of his own to live upon. For lands of their
nature are equally divided among the male children, or,
if there be no sonnes, among the daughters. By vertue
of this also they are at full age, and enter upon their
inheritance, when they come to be fifteen yeares old ; and
lawful it is for them to alienate, and make it over to anyone,
either by gift or by sale without the Lord's consent. By this
likewise the sonnes, though their parents were condemned
for theft, succeede them neverthelesse in such kind of lands."

Modern historians pooh-pooh chroniclers' tales of the
success of the men of Kent in dealing with William the
Conqueror, but cannot deny that Kent did in fact retain
under Norman rule many laws and customs which
differentiated it from the rest of England, and which
may have been a heritage from the Jutes, or may have
been derived from Celtic ancestors. Moreover, as late
as in the reign of Queen Victoria, when an Act of Parliament

was passed commuting certain manorial rights, a special clause exempted from the operation of the Act "the custom of gavelkind as the same now exists and prevails in the county of Kent."

The law of gavelkind naturally tended to the distribution of wealth, and may have contributed to the general prosperity which the people of Kent have always been reported to enjoy. Under Anglo-Saxon rule the wergyld (*i.e.*, price to be paid if he were killed) of a freeman of Kent was two and a half times that of his neighbour the West Saxon, and our Kentish countrymen of to-day are well aware of their long standing as men of substance and like to quote the rhyme :—

> " A knight of Cales,
>   A gentleman of Wales
>   And a laird of the north countree,
>   A Yeoman of Kent,
>   With his yearly rent
>   Will buy them out all three."

This rhyme dates from Elizabethan days, and the expression " knight of Cales " refers to knighthoods given by the Queen to various gentlemen who had supported the Earl of Essex in a project which was equivalent to a " commando " raid on Calais (Cales).

Ancient rhymes have been handed down from generation to generation in Kent and are still popular, some of them being of historic interest, others descriptive, and even childishly abusive, jingles which indicate local rivalries. We have, for instance :—

> " *Naughty Ashford, surly Wye*
> *Poor Kennington, hard by.*"

> " *Dirty Charing lies in a hole,*
> *It had but one bell and that was stole.*"

> " *Ickham, Wickham and Wingham women,*
> *Sat upon Littlebourne Hill a-spinning.*"

> " *Rye, Romney and Hythe for wealth without health,*
> *The Downs for health with povertee ;*
> *But you shall find both health and wealth*
> *From Foreland Head to Knole and Lee.*"

Games and frolics on the village greens are suggested by the old counting-out rhyme,

> "*Ickham, pickham,*
> *Penny Wickham,*
> *Cockalorum Jay,*
> *Eggs, butter, cheese, bread,*
> *Hick, stick, stone dead.*"

Village greens have played a large part in the life of the county, whether as the scene of meetings held by Jack Cade and his like, or as the " playstoles " whereon in mediæval days companies of village players " showed their May," and delighted their neighbours with mumming and acting of " interludes." For the last four hundred years or so these lovely greens have been in Summer the site of weekly cricket matches, many of which have provided satisfactory subjects for local conversation for, at any rate, fifty years ! In 1672 a parson complained that " Maidstone was formerly a very prophane town, insomuch that (before 1640) I have seen morrice dancing, cudgel playing, stoolball, cricket and many other sports, openly and publicly on the Lord's day." In the village near which I made my home, however, it had been the custom in the " good old days " for the parson himself, clad in his surplice, to open the cricket season on Easter Sunday by bowling the first ball on the village green directly after morning service. In the early years of the nineteenth century village cricket was frequently played for large wagers, but the incident which was most affectionately remembered in our particular village was the occasion in 1872 when three famous cricket playing inhabitants, aged over seventy, advertised in " Bell's Life " that they took " the liberty of giving a public challenge to play a match of cricket with any three of England of not less average age than seventy-three. They will make the match for any amount not exceeding £100."

" Grim and gay " was Kent, always ready to defend her ancient liberties, always ready to claim the forefront of the battle, always ready for a bit of fun. Grim and gay she is to-day, with land more productive than ever before ; with rich pastures, fine corn and bean fields, and many woods; with hop gardens greatly increased in number since they were first introduced about the year 1552; with orchards and fruit a-plenty, and particularly cherries, " which being brought out of Pontus into Italie in the 608 yeare after the foundation of Rome, and in the 120 yeare after translated into Britaine, prosper here exceeding well; the trees being planted in a direct manner, one against another by square, most pleasant to behold."

Most pleasant to behold is all the countryside of Kent, and though her story has been written in many books, it is written still more fully in her fields, her roads, her ancient houses, her villages, and in the character of her people. Outwardly peaceful, Kent has weathered many storms; always prosperous, she has nevertheless known times which were, in the words of the Anglo-Saxon chronicle " swinkful and sorrowful," but Kent remains serenely Kent. Before the birth of Christ her people stood armed, waiting and watching. In Saxon days when Kent was Christian, but much of England was still pagan, the battle cry was " For Kent and Christendom." To-day, nearly 2,000 years after the death of Christ, the people of Kent stand waiting and armed again, but going on with their daily work as steadily and cheerfully as if they were not within sight, sound, and quick news, of some of the most grim events of history.

Invincible of spirit are they, whether they be " men of Kent " born east and south-east of the Medway, or " Kentish men " born to the river's west. " England of England " is Kent.

THE
WAY OF THE DOWNS

By WINIFRED A. GORICK

THE long green coaches slid away from the platform.
The 10.33 had been so packed with people leaving the
town, Miss Grafton expected to find Terminus Road
deserted. Crowds of shoppers, however, were gathered
round the bus stop just outside the station, while knots
of children from Old Town, laden with spades and buckets,
were making their way down to the beach.

She had to wait until she had turned into the residential
area before the unreal silence, which she knew was
descending on the town like an evening mist, stole around
her. The grounds of the boys' college were deserted,
the windows of the headmaster's house shuttered and
unresponsive. St. Joan's was at the corner. Yes, the
boarders had left there, too. She wondered if any of the
day girls would still attend.

Her own school overlooked the sea, and Beachy Head
and the Downs provided a background of serene Sussex

beauty. As her footsteps crunched up the gravel of
the drive she could hear Mary in the drawing-room. A
bee was in the geraniums, its low humming mingling
with that of the Hoover, giving a false air of activity
to the house. The door of the library was ajar. The
room smelt stuffy, and her footsteps echoed as she crossed
the parquet floor to open the window. It had been high
tide when she had bathed at seven that morning, but
now the rocks were beginning to show their green ribs
through the fringe of surf. She could see old Benton,
from the Pilot Inn, picking his way among the boulders
at the base of the cliff. He would expect her to take
some of his prawns, just as usual. " Just as usual," with
the school pupil-less and the low rumble of gunfire coming
across the Channel. The news was bad. One could
understand parents growing restless. She had hoped to
have finished the term, but that interview with the tall
figure in khaki in her study last Friday had precipitated
events. For a moment she had thought he was the
father of one of the girls. He had been very charming.
" The Government needs your school, Miss Grafton.
I am sorry. Can you possibly arrange to hand it over
within a week ? You will have to find alternative premises
further inland." Evacuation—a word she hated.

She leaned her head against the window frame. Well,
the girls had gone. The last six had left that morning.
She had felt too numbed to make immediate arrangements
for re-opening. Perhaps she would do so in the Autumn,
at the moment she could not think. The silence of the
room hurt. Her throat felt tight. She went into the
kitchen and cut herself a sandwich. The pantry was cool
and green, " like one of the caves at the Gap," she found
herself inconsequently thinking, and then knew what
she was going to do.

She changed into a dress and picked up a sun hat. The
Downs flanked the town on the west, and the top of the
road ended abruptly in a white chalky path. To the right
a broad, tree-shaded avenue wound round the green bowl
of the golf course, then continued on into the red-roofed
town. The chalky path skirted the copse growing round

the disused reservoirs, and cut into the spongey turf of Warren Hill. The climb was steep, but she took it at a good pace. Passing the ruined shepherd's hut, she made for the dew pond hidden in the circle of gorse bushes. She remembered that Sally, the cocker she had fifteen years ago, first discovered it for her. She had gone racing on ahead, and disappeared into the bushes on a rabbit hunt, to return wet and barking. It had been a hot Summer that year, and the water in the pond was low. The sheep had used it, and she thought of how she cleaned Sally's nose of the little red ticks that had burrowed into her skin. The pond was full to-day, a placid blue circle in a concrete saucer. Strange how these concrete settings became a part of the Downs. The hills had a knack of absorbing man's work, making the symmetry of a dew pond's artificial basin more satisfying than the hoof-marked mud round the edges of the few ponds left untouched.

The old lighthouse, too, had grown into the Downs, its sturdy walls rubbing their chins into the prickly gorse bushes that bearded the hill. Even the water tower at Friston had been accepted. Square-shouldered and massive it broke into the horizon, a modern beacon of man's progress. Yes, useful buildings were adopted by the Downs. They trusted the grey stone farms and, in grateful return for the farmer's combing and grooming of their fields, threw a mantle of russet lichen over the roofs of barns and house alike. She felt that the hills loved tossing golden manes of corn in the August breezes, and were glad to give refuge to the homes of their brown-skinned grooms. But man could go too far, and what neither she, nor the Downs, could stomach, was the spate of red villas pouring in unhappy confusion along the brow and over the sides of the distant hill. In vain did the owners mow their lawns and plant their flowers, the hills waged battle with weapons of wind and thistle and dust and chalk. She had watched the tussle with a quiet satisfaction, long after the first fury at the desecration of her Downland had settled into passive resentment. The hills could afford to wait. They knew the day would

N

come when the villas would crumble away and the yellow gorse would hide the scars their foundations had made.

Leaving the villas behind her, Miss Grafton turned towards the Gap. Her thoughts were gradually taking shape. The school was finished. She had no desire to gather its threads together and to transplant it to some village far inland. She had never been able to express in her expensively printed prospectus the inner springs of strength in her curriculum. How could she explain the healing of Janet Halliday ? She could not write down, as in a cookery recipe, " Take one reserved, embittered child, offspring of rich divorced parents. Place her in a small bedroom, with a large window, facing sea and Downs. Let the rhythm of the sea cleanse her soul from smallness, let the sense of peace and strength of the hills be drawn into her lungs with every breath. Give her games and work and laughter with other girls, give her moments of silence in the school chapel where she may learn the spirit of worship. Let her whiten her shoes with the dust of chalky paths, and let her wander in the hills in the company of a chosen friend. Let the silence of the chapel and of the Downs become as one in her mind, so that a bottomless well of faith is formed within her, from which she may draw a *living* philosophy."

She had taken the Downs and the sea, and the faith which they had strengthened, and built thereon her school. A school elsewhere would be meaningless for her.

The smugglers' path she had been following ended abruptly at the cliff edge. She sat down and took out her lunch. By the time she was methodically peeling her orange she had come to a decision. She felt as though her mind were divided into compartments. In one was a deep burning resentment against God for allowing her school to close down. In another was her ingrained faith in His ultimate wisdom, and a realization that war was of man's making, not God's. For the moment, however, it was easier to blame an intangible God, despite His reality to her, than a collective humanity which she had always found so warm-hearted. From the Officer who was taking over her school, down to old Benton

with his prawns, individuals were so attractive, kindly
and lovable, it was difficult to say, with any degree of
accuracy, "You are responsible for this impasse in my
life." This compartment of her mind must be closed
for the time being. She would open it and sort things
out one evening when she had leisure. Already the
decision had become so real she could visualize the future.
She could not leave Sussex. She would take a cottage
in one of the nearby villages, Alfriston, Jevington,
Wilmington, it did not matter exactly where, save that
she would like to be near the sea. Later on, perhaps,
she could do some private tutoring but, for the moment,
she would give up every responsibility and just live at
peace in the Downs.

She stood up and looked along the coastline. She
could see five of the Seven Cliffs which were linked with
Beachy Head. Was anywhere lovelier than this southern
bastion of England? Sussex expressed for her a code
of living; here nature was simplified into a perfection of
line and colour. The hills rose in soft folds, long curves
of soundless music. The cliffs were cleanly sculptured
from the white chalk, their walls, smooth and straight,
making a dazzling barrier to sea and invader alike. Only
the gulls, glorying in their freedom of movement, presaged
the new battles of the limitless sky. Far below, black
hunches of rock showed through the sand and shingle.
Black, white, green, blue, sunshine, shadow, every line
clearly defined, no confusion, no fussiness, dignified,
courteous, proud yet simple, that was Sussex. Suddenly,
she realized the depth of her love for the Downs and all
they embodied. She could bear to lose her school, but
these hills and headlands claimed her for their own. As
they had cast their spell over farmstead and concrete,
so had they taken her, making her one with their bigness
of vision, one with their simplicity of line and directness
of colour.

It started to rain as she turned inland, and small clouds
were scudding across the sky as though anxious to join
the mass of cumulus forming over Wilmington. She
passed the gate of Friston Church, and she pictured the

cool interior and the stone effigies to a couple, prominent in their day. There they had knelt for centuries with their children, also with bowed heads, meekly kneeling beneath them. Beneath the prayer stool, tiny stone effigies in swaddling clothes perpetuated the memory of the two babies who had died in infancy, a picture of family life in earlier days. She thought of Janet, with her modern assortment of four parents. Was this the civilization we were bent on saving?

It was nearly six o'clock as she dropped into the town. The hills rose in a dark wall behind her. The wind was blowing from the sea in vicious gusts, angrily whipping into shreds the peacefully rising smoke from the chimneys. Dr. Thomas was coming out of a small house as she passed. They were close friends, but he hardly smiled as he saw her.

" Can I give you a lift? You've heard the news, of course? "

His plain face was puckered in bewilderment.

" I can't believe it, but we're leaving France. Every boat has been called out. Our men coming back home in the middle of a battle! It can't be true. The port's Dunkirk. France is falling. God knows what will happen next."

The news swept through the town. Stunned, incredulous, for a moment holiday makers, boarding-house keepers, hotel proprietors, shop-keepers, residents rich and poor, stood aghast. Then they awakened and faced reality. Children and invalids were sent off to the country. With minds freed the housewives turned round, rolled up their sleeves, and set to work. After the first moment of dismayed horror a glorious, humorous, activity came into being. The white bathing huts were dragged up from the beaches. Turned on their backs, with their entrances staring at the sky, they were made into barricades all over the town. Soldiers and civilians dug deep into the shingle and filled sandbags with the pebbles. These, in turn, were dropped into the open mouths of the bathing huts. New recruits, with the soft inexperienced fingers of their boyhood, fixed barbed wire along the beach. The tide came in overnight, laughed at their fumbling efforts, and swept their work away, The old martello tower was draped in net, and soldiers, singing in the sunshine, stuck sprigs of evergreen between the brickwork. Had Germany struck then, she would have found a town of Davids armed with but little else than the stones found on their beaches.

But Germany did not strike and, as the months went by, the town at the foot of the Downs became fringed with iron teeth instead of slings.

In her cottage at Wilmington Miss Grafton waited. Her days were busy. A.R.P. duties, Red Cross work at the Institute, a dozen small activities filled the hours, but she could neither recapture her peace nor her happiness. She missed the daily intercourse with keen, intelligent young minds. She missed the spaciousness of the school-rooms and felt, at times, as though the walls of the cottage were an early tomb, pressing in and encompassing her, until she had to step out into the lane and walk close to the open fields. Even on the Downs she could not find peace. She had spent her whole life in service to the young, striving to build constructively, waging a war against the stark materialism of the age. She felt that adults had served youth so meanly, giving money in place of love and homelife and faith. Youth had always borne the brunt of the cynicism of the previous generation, and now youth once more was being sacificed to the selfishness of the old.

She was glad to find that John, at the vicarage, wanted to learn German. They spent the mornings together. He was young and fair, eager for the day when he could join the Air Force. His picture of a post-war Europe was a neatly-patterned one. He seemed to think all Nazi supporters would be killed by the R.A.F. bombs, and that the young Germans left would quickly see reason—the reasoning of the British—and would gladly help to build a saner world. " That's why I must learn German. You must talk to a chap in his own lingo."

Day and night the air was heavy with the drone of bombers. Young pilots would practice over the roofs of the village. Walking along the ridge at the top of the Wilmington Giant, she suddenly had to throw herself to the ground as a Wellington cleared the brow with only a yard or two to spare. The planes would roar over the hill tops, their great black shadows racing across the fields of corn. By day, the Downs were vibrant with the teeming life of the strange new aviary camouflaged on the plain. Only at night could she recapture, for brief moments, the timeless spirit of peace. The hills regained their right proportions, no longer dwarfed by the impudent machines that jeered at their heights in the sunshine. Firle Beacon stood high and mysterious in the moonlight, the Wilmington Giant leaned on his two sticks and peered across the plain, dominant on his hillside once more.

At dusk she would take sandwiches and coffee to the scattered searchlight crews. She would tell them of the Downs, of the men who buried their dead in the tumuli by which the crews were camped. She told them of the ghosts that peopled Horselunges Manor and the Mint House at Pevensey, and she took them down to the Priory at Wilmington and out to the Abbey at Battle. Sitting in the twilight, the men forgot the tall figure of the English schoolmistress. She became a voice, the voice of the Downs telling always of men who came up to the hills to work, to worship, and to find freedom. And the hills accepted them all ; the monks who tilled the abbey fields, the soldiers who lighted the beacon on Firle, the men in khaki who tended the great torches that patterned the sky with tapering fingers of exquisite light. She passed on the message of timeless endurance ; but peace was not in her own soul.

She was awakened one morning by the sound of planes. The low room was filled with the throbbing of the engines. She went to the window and leaned out. The sky was streaked with the pale green of early dawn. Great black-bodied planes were landing and taking off in a continuous stream. They would pass over the cottage and then roar out across the Channel. This was no ordinary practice. The whole world seemed full of noise, the very Downs were stirring, sending out echoes that surely throbbed through the whole of England. Hour after hour, the exodus continued, and she was impotent to discover what it foretold. At last it was time for the news bulletin. Eagerly she switched on her wireless set. The calm, detached voice of the announcer described the scene that was happening at her cottage door. " This is a message to the people of France. We are making a raid, but not an invasion. The hour of your liberation is near."

Later, the planes began to return. Tiny silver gnats, they appeared over the Channel, some flying boldly in formation, others limping home with their wounds. She lay on the top of Windover Hill, the great Sussex Weald behind her, counting the squadrons. She became absorbed in her task, thrilling when the groups numbered full strength. She felt part of the battle. It was good to be on the offensive again, sending out troops to combat the enemy on his own ground. A low rumble came over the water, a continuous thunder. She had not heard that sound for two years, the noise of gunfire in France.

She packed up her lunch the next morning. The exhilaration of the previous day had left her tired and depressed. The Dieppe raid was over. England had spat fire, and had then drawn in her claws. She was crouching ready to spring. The young could prepare for action, but the old, like herself, must wait. Next month there would be work to do. She would help with the fruit harvest at Hailsham, but for the moment there was nothing. She dropped down by Snaphill Barn. The valley was a great sheet of whispering yellow corn. Changing her mind, she turned to her right and climbed up again towards Seaford Head. She crossed the bridge at Exceat and followed the river. There was a slight mist on the hills, but the sun was breaking through and she thought it would be hot. The footpath ran under an overhanging bank. The field above had been furrowed to the very edge, and the corn and the poppies had spilled over on to the rough ground beneath. A grey boulder had fallen across the path. A gust of wind blew past her, and suddenly the boulder moved. Startled, she

went up to it. Billowing across the ground was an opened
parachute. Still attached to the harness, a quiet figure
in grey uniform lay crumpled up on the green path. Miss
Grafton stood still, an unreasoning fear holding her back.
The valley was silent. Then she leant over the body.
He was little more than a boy, perhaps nineteen or twenty.
His eyes were open. They were blue. His hair was
straight and childishly flaxen. Across the breast of his
uniform was a reddish-brown stain.

He was oddly like John at the vicarage, yet curiously
like Hans who had so proudly shown her round Munich
only four years ago. John who wanted to go to Germany,
first to kill evil, and then to teach his contemporaries how
to live. Hans who wanted to come to England to establish
his ideology. Youth striving for an ideal; yet her
generation had done nothing to give youth a sure
foundation for life. It had been just callous and selfish.

Kneeling by the dead boy, a mist slowly lifted from
her brain. Her thoughts became defined and vigorous,
stepping out of the morass of self pity of the last two
years, as she had seen the cliffs loom suddenly sharp and
clear through a morning fog. The erstwhile happiness
for which she had longed could never be hers again.
What right had she to claim it ? She, with countless
others of her age, had been given twenty years in which
to create peace. When they failed, she had thrust the
blame upon God. She had thought to wash her hands
in the clear streams that flowed through the hills.

With a startling clarity she saw the failure of the wasted
years. One, in death, with the English lads who had
crashed in France the day before, the silent grey-clad
figure lay there, a mute sacrifice to the blindness of those
who had led his world. The hills, in their wisdom, would
bend over to receive him ; he had come unasked to their
valley. Lying there on the soft turf, with the poppies
flaunting their red crowns above him, he was now beyond
nationality. In a day or two they would place him deep
within Sussex soil.

Miss Grafton rose from her knees, her lips straightening
into a determined line. She had been seeking for peace

in the Downs, demanding it in return for giving them her allegiance. The hills had withheld it. Their spell could not be laid on the whimsical sentimentality of a country cottage. Peace was not bought so easily. They demanded faith and service.

She felt as though she were standing on a headland with the past two years rolling away beneath her feet. Etched in the clearly defined colours of the Downs she saw herself, self-centred, cowardly, demanding of life yet refusing to give, boasting a faith which would not stand the test of a new beginning. She realized the futility of the two wasted years, fumbling with work for which she was not trained ; her cottage and her love for the hills an escape from the responsibilities for which she was really called.

She turned towards Wilmington, a new humility and a new confidence filling her heart. She was eager for action, anxious to make restitution for her failure of the past. On her writing desk was a letter from the Headmistress of St. Joan's, long since evacuated to Wales, inviting her help and offering her a partnership. With a gesture of impatience she had thrown the letter aside, hardly bothering to read it. She knew now her answer must be one of acceptance. The urgent questioning of youth must be heeded, and, with the quiet satisfaction of the teacher, she realized the Downs had given her a knowledge which she must not fail to pass on.

"THE MUMMERS." TAKEN FROM AN OLD PICTURE

AN OLD MUMMER AT THE CHEQUERS, WHEELER END

By H. HARMAN

IT was Christmas week and the "Chequers," Wheeler End, was full. The conversation turned to the subject of the season's festivities, and to the jolly times the people used to have on the commons. One or two of the oldest lamented that the old traditional spirit had died out, and that the celebrations of recent years were not comparable to those of forty or fifty years previous. Among the company was Abel Collins, the last surviving member of the Wheeler End Mummers.

He said that in his time the young men, on the approach of Christmas, were full of joyous anticipation at the prospect of visiting the neighbouring farms and villages to give the play which had been handed down in the hamlet from time immemorial. He then went on further to state that when the dark days of November had arrived, the band of Mummers used to commence their practice in the kiln on Cadmore End Common. On certain nights of the week they met, when with the outhouse dimly lighted by a tallow candle or two, each performer went through his part until he could do it well. There was always one more present than the number required, to fill any vacancy that might arise. At Christmas they visited, and wherever they performed they received a welcome.

When the conversation had proceeded further, the Mummer was asked whether he could remember the words, and he replied that he thought he was able to do so, although so many years had elapsed since he had taken part in its performance.

Standing in the centre of the tap-room he went through the whole play without the slightest hesitation, accompanying each character with suitable actions.

* * * * *

(The Wheeler End version, here appended, was played by nine persons, the characters being as follows :

1. Roomer, director of the ceremony.
2. King George, representing St. George, the Patron Saint of England.
3. Bull Slasher, King George's opponent.
4. Doctor.
5. Jack Finney.
6. Beelzebub.
7. Miss Fly.
8. Father Christmas.
9. Big Head.

Supernumeraries.

The usual routine was for the company to stand outside the door of the cottage or inn, and when all was ready, Roomer entered with a broom and proceeded to clear a convenient space for the acting. He then called in the actors, one by one, who then performed their parts in proper sequence. The costumes worn were of a very grotesque description, one at least being an old discarded

tunic of the Bucks Militia, to which many of the young
fellows of Wheeler End used to belong.

The reader will understand that Mr. Collins impersonated
each player in turn.   Every time he bade one to enter,
he turned to the tap-room door, after a pause he turned
to the company and performed the part.   The whole play
is here given as it was performed with interpolations.)

Bursting into the room with a broom in his hand, he
proceeds to clear the centre of the floor from all imaginary
obstructions, and at the same time in a commanding
voice, impersonating Roomer, shouts :

" A room !   A room fur me and mi broom,
    And all mi jovial men behind !
    I must have room and I WULL have room,
    All round, this Christmas time."

Calls :   " Come in, King George."

(Enter King George.)

KING GEORGE :

" In comes King George—that noble man,
    The fust that e'er took su-urd in hand.
    Show me the man that bids me stand,
    I'll cut him down with my courageous hand !
    I'll cut him up !   I'll cut him down !
    I'll cut him up as small and as numerous as flies,
    And send him to the cook-shop to meeak mince-pies !
    Mince-pies hot !   Mince-pies cold !
    Mince-pies in the pot nine days old !

ROOMER (in a very subdued and cautionary manner) :

" Hush !   Hush !   King George !   do-ant be so hot,
    You do-ant know what kind of men outside I've got."

(Bull Slasher enters.)

" In comes this valiant soldier bold,
    Bull Slasher is mi nee-am.
    With a long su-urd buckled bi mi side,
    I'm bound to win the gee-am.
    A challenge to battle, I ull call
    To see which uv us an the ground shull fall,
    Now guard yur head and mind mi blows,
    Look artur yur feeace and mind yur noo-az (Nose)."

The fight now takes place, Mr. Collins taking the role of King George against his imaginary opponent, Bull Slasher. Holding a walking stick to represent a sword, and assuming a defiant attitude, he stood with his back against the tap-room door. Then, slightly crouching, and looking fixedly in front, he, little by little, moves onward along the floor. When he reached the centre he sprang to the assault on his imaginary enemy. He lunged, he thrusted, he parried and struck the tap-room table some resounding thwacks. He then retreated as if he were hard pressed, and then recovering himself, advanced up the floor again, shouting and hurling defiance. Reaching the centre he gradually retreated again, parrying and thrusting until he was driven back to his original position at the door. Suddenly dropping his guard he fell headlong up the centre of the floor, and lay stretched out his full length of six feet and over.

He now groans and his face assumes the features of a sorely stricken man. After struggling a little, he becomes quiet and softly murmurs : " Oh dear ! I be bad ! I be wounded ! " with other exclamations of a similar nature. Remaining thus prostrate for a little while, it gave him time to recover his breath and compose the agitation caused by his excessive exertion.

He now rises, and again facing the company exclaims :
(ROOMER) :
" What would I give for a jolly noble doctur ! "
" Ten pounds ! Twenty pounds ! "
(VOICE OUTSIDE) :
" Twenty pounds' my fee."
ROOMER :
" Come in doctur ! "
" Doctur, doctur, come away ;
  Doctur, doctur, don't delay,
  Doctur, doctur, do yur part,
  King George is wounded close to the heart."
                    (*Doctor enters.*)
DOCTOR :
" In comes this hickety-pickety doctur,
  Can't say doctur, but Hoctur,

Bound to cure all dis-eeases.
Jest what my physic pleeases.
Molly-grubs, scolly-grubs, rantanses, smallpox and the gout,
Pains within and pains without."

(He now impersonates the doctor.)

Kneeling down on the floor by his imaginary patient, he looks into his face, sounds him in various parts of the body, and takes on a very serious countenance. "Ah!" he says, "you be bad! What can I do fur ye! Wha's the matter wi ye? I ull cu-ur ye, that e ull. I a cu-urd a good many worse than you in mi time. Now then, opun yur mouth and shet yur eyes and see what Uncle Tom sends ye! Hee-urs a pill! Teeak that and gollop it down! Tha'ull tickle ye up if nothing else ull! Tha's the stuff! Can't ye feel it a-dooin ye good? E can see ye a-gittin better! Ah, he's neeurly well."

(Stands and shouts.)

"Rise King George and fight again!"

(The combat is resumed.)

The old Mummer goes through the same actions as before, advancing and retreating, thrusting and smiting, and inadvertently making the tap-room tables resound with some mighty smacks. But the exertion is too great for the combat to be continued, and just in the middle of a furious bout he again falls and lies apparently motionless except for his rapid breathing. In a moment or two he groans and then when his breath is more quiet, lies his full length along the floor as rigid as death. After a while he rises and stands facing the door.

Shouts: "Come in Jack Finney."

(Jack Finney enters.)

JACK FINNEY. "Ugh, my neeam's Mr. Finney. The leeast you could a done would a bin to call me John!"

ROOMER. "Then what can you do?"

JACK FINNEY. "More than you or any other man I a sin yit awhile. Cure this man if he ant bin dead above a fortnight. Had a very serious ceeas come to me a few days agoo."

ROOMER.   " What was that ? "

JACK FINNEY.   " Had a sparrow come to me wi the toothache."

ROOMER.   " And how did you cu-ur it ? "

JACK FINNEY.   " Pulled his head awf and smartly throwed his body in a ditch."

(Mr. Collins again kneels and impersonates Jack Finney treating King George.)

He examines the imaginary body, turns it, looks into the face, feels the pulse and then pretends to give medicine. During these actions he makes various remarks and after a while exclaims : " He's a-gittin better. He's gittin ovur it. I can see him move. Mi medicine a done it. He ull soon be alright. Hullo ! he's neeurly well."

The old Mummer then stands, and in a commanding voice shouts :

" Rise King George, and fight no more ! "

He then proceeds normally to the end of the play.

ROOMER :

" Come in Beelzebub."

BEELZEBUB :

" In comes old Beelzebub,
    In my hand I carry a club,
    And bi mi side a drippin pan,
    Don't ye think I'm a nice ole man ! "

ROOMER :

" Come in Miss Fly."

MISS FLY :

" In comes I,
    As light as a fly.
    Got no money,
    And what cares I."

ROOMER :

" Come in Father Christmas."

FATHER CHRISTMAS :

" In comes ole Father Christmas,
    Ant got long to stay.
    But e hopes as you'll remember me,
    Afu-ur e goos away."

ROOMER :
   " Come in Big Head."
   BIG HEAD :
   " In comes ole Big Head,
     With my big head and little wit ;
     Mi head's so big,
     And mi wit's so small,
     So e a brought mi fiddle,
     To pleease ye all."

Taking up the walking stick and bending his elbow, the old Mummer sawed on his upper arm in imitation of a fiddler. At the same time he, in an agile manner, danced round the tap-room accompanying himself by humming the melody of the hornpipe that was accustomed to be played. He went up and down, and round and round in a surprising manner for one of his age. This, however, he could not keep up for long, as he again began to show distinct effects of his unusual activity. His breath became short and he was at last obliged to recline exhausted and breathless on one of the tap-room tables. " Ah ! " he exclaimed, after a rest. " This ood nivver a happund fifty yeeur agoo, but e be now a good deal ovur seventy, and so e can't expect to do as e used to. E could then a gone through wi it and nivver felt a bit out a breath ; but tis jest a bit too much fur me now to do all the parts bi miself."·

After the lapse of a minute or two he regained his composure and then returned to his seat.

The company was as stolid as ever all through the acting, the only demonstration being at the end, when one said, " Well done, Abel ! " but throughout, their appreciation of their fellow villager was visibly shown by their rapt attention, and by the smiles which occasionally passed over their countenances. And no wonder, for the histrionic ability displayed by the old Mummer was a revelation, coming as it did from one who had lived all his life on Wheeler End Common.